# Write-a-thon

# Write-a-thon

*How to Conduct a Writing Marathon
in Your Third- to Fifth-Grade Class*

## Susie Wilde

bee line
BOOKS

Heinemann
Portsmouth, NH

**Beeline Books**

An imprint of Heinemann
A division of Reed Elsevier Inc.
361 Hanover Street
Portsmouth, NH 03801-3912
*Offices and agents throughout the world*

We are grateful to the following publishers for granting permission to reprint material from previously published works: Excerpt from *The New King* by Doreen Rappaport. © 1995 by Doreen Rapport, text. Used by permission of Dial Books for Young Readers, a division of Penguin Books USA Inc. Excerpt from *The Frog Prince Continued* by Jon Sciezska. © 1991 by Jon Sciezska, text. Used by permission of Viking Penguin, a division of Penguin Books USA Inc.

Acquiring Editor: Cheryl Kimball
Production Editor: Renée M. Nicholls
Cover and Interior Design: Greta D. Sibley
Decorative Embellishments: Stephanie Peterson and Greta D. Sibley
Manufacturing Coordinator: Louise Richardson

**Library of Congress Cataloguing-in-Publication Data**
Wilde, Susie, 1951–
    Write-a-thon : how to conduct a writing marathon in your third- to fifth-grade class / Susie Wilde.
        p.  cm.
    Includes bibliographical references (p. ).
    ISBN 0-435-08141-1 (alk. paper)
    1. English language––Composition and exercises––Study and teaching (Elementary)––United States.   2. Group work in education––United States.   3. Education, Elementary––Activity programs––United States.
    I. Title.
LB1576.W48765   1996
372.6\23\044––dc21
                                 96-49058
                                   CIP

Printed in the United States of America on acid-free paper
99 98 97 EB 1 2 3 4 5 6

*To Ron, my life coach,*
*and to Ben and Emily, who keep my pace steady*

# Contents

# *Acknowledgments*

The author wishes to thank the athletes and coaches who blazed the write-a-thon way. A special thanks to coaches Marrero, Colomb, Frase, Stuckey, West, Wipper, Penn, and Peg. The author is grateful to the Friends of Weymouth, an incredible aid station. A gold medal goes to Jackie Ogburn, Carol Henderson, Laura Sweeny, Ginger Knowlton, and Jane Tuttle, who cheered me from the sidelines, and to Cheryl Kimball, who helped me cross the finish line.

# *Introduction: The Warm-Up*

My writing with children began with my own writing. During a twelve-year teaching respite, I devoted myself to discovering my own writing process, producing twenty-seven books for children. When I came back into the classroom, I wanted children to experience the magic, surprise, and joy of the creative process I'd found.

I saw the same problems arise again and again in students' writing. They pasted cardboard characters on a meaningless plot and then, without a sense of what was driving the story, began to wander off in all kinds of directions until neither story, character, nor writing had value to them. The words were empty and wouldn't mean much to readers. And it was hard work! Even children who were more capable writers—usually the ones who were readers—had a difficult time negotiating the twists and turns of their own fiction.

I wondered how children could learn to write when they didn't understand the process. Beginning writers learn early to "show, not tell," to reveal story through dialogue and action. In the classroom, I twisted this adage to mean showing and talking children through the writing process rather than telling them to write and leaving them to their own resources. During such a collaborative writing process, we begin a story with character development and move through plot and on to resolution together.

Good stories come from understanding a character and then listening to the story that character has to tell. As a group we define a character by suggesting a long list of characters, voting to select one, and then exploring that choice. Through a series of questions, we learn

- the character's motivation
- the conflict
- the resolution to that conflict.

All this is accomplished in short segments of time over several days. During the process students would often suggest ideas that didn't have relevance to the story or fit with the character we'd described. I found in classroom after classroom that they needed structure and questioning to promote wondering. They needed encouragement to keep them from putting forth pat or implausible responses and from racing to be finished instead of really exploring. I helped them build a sense of responsibility to the character and story by continually questioning their choices. Children need help reaching the stories locked within them. Good writing means imagining thoughtfully, constructing an internal logic, and questioning choices.

This questioning led again and again to poignant discussion. In one third-grade classroom for example, we created Storm, a lonely child who is misunderstood by his parents and peers. We'd worked hard to portray him as powerless and victimized. His only power came when he turned into a panther because of a bite he'd received as a child.

"How did he act with his friends?" I asked.

"He clawed and bit them," one child said.

"He killed them," a classmate added and others agreed quickly.

"I don't buy it," I told them. "That doesn't fit with the way we described him as a caring and hurt child. He wouldn't want to hurt others because he knows too well what hurt feels like." When I held them accountable, they could move away from cartoon responses into really thinking about what power meant. At the story's resolution, we described Storm's conflict and gave him a different kind of power.

> When a mean bunch of kids pushed him down, took his lunch money and ripped up his homework, Storm would find privacy and then transform into a panther where he could roar out his anger.

One day a pack of bullies tripped him. When he fell to the ground, they kicked at him, calling him a wimp the whole time. Storm found a quiet place and became a panther, unsheathing his giant claws and scratching at a tree until his anger went away.

Storm was finally relaxed and ready to return to face the cruelty of the kids at school. As he ran through the fields, a kid spotted him.

Full of fear, some children screamed while others ran to get help. Almost instantly, everyone at the school knew a panther was running wild in the long grasses behind the school.

Someone ran to the principal for help. The principal called 911 and everyone from the community came. There were police, hunters, SPCA and zoo trainers with tranquilizer guns, the rescue squad, reporters and hundreds of parents.

The parents rushed around the school, finding their children. Storm's mom and dad couldn't find their son. They began to panic and dashed frantically around the school trying to locate him.

Storm was just as desperate to find a way out of the problem. He paced around the school roaring. When he trotted close to the playground, a zoo keeper aimed a tranquilizer gun, fired, hit Storm in the leg, and the panther fell to the ground, unconscious.

When Storm woke, he was surrounded by children and adults. Every single person was silent with amazement.

From that day, Storm became the most popular kid at the school. He was nicknamed Panther Boy and everyone respected him because he got his power from deep inside.

These are the kinds of questions with which writers grapple and whose clear resolution they rejoice over. I want all children to have the glorious feeling of authoring meaningful stories.

While I believe in the power of collaborative writing as a way to begin to understand story, ultimately we want children to discover their own writing voices. The write-a-thon was born of a desire to help students take the learning of collaborative writing and apply it to their individual stories.

Again and again in collaborative writing, I'd seen how there were crucial moments in writing in which children would pull away from the logical world they had established and move in different directions that threatened the sense of the story they were creating. They'd suddenly decide to explore a tangent that ran contrary to the character they'd described or focus on a detail that moved the story in a confusing direction. Children who are beginning to write need help thinking. While challenging them opened up great discussion in collaborative writing, I wondered how to help them transfer the skills they'd shown as a team into their individual stories.

The write-a-thon gives students two days during which they are individually coached and checked as each story evolves. The write-a-thon is a bridge from group to individual writing. It has all the elements of fun and presents the techniques of writing in a different context. It is designed to be led by many coaches—not just one teacher—so that children can constantly be heard and comforted and encouraged on this new playing field. The coaches are, for the most part, parents, which means that home is supporting school. The write-a-thon acknowledges parents as teachers, allows opportunity for children and parents to play together in an educational setting, and encourages a feeling of success at the project's end.

This book is meant as a starting place for teachers and contains loads of suggestions to help you imagine how you would put together your own writing marathon. Remember that you are the coach who understands your team best. Pick what works, transform what doesn't, and share your ideas with others. Coaching has its moments of sweat and tears, but the triumph is sweeter than you can imagine!

 *Write-a-thon*

**CHAPTER**

**1**

# Training Your Athletes

As the teacher, you will act as the write-a-thon's head coach. The job of head coach begins with training the team (your students). During the training process both writing and running athletes

- Experiment with information and techniques
- Develop style and form
- Define and apply themselves to the tasks at hand
- Establish a routine for practicing
- Test skills and limits
- Develop improved strategies
- Understand new facets of themselves

Running athletes train alone in most cases, but this is a pretty overwhelming list for children to master. That's why coaching needs to begin with the supportive process of collaborative writing.

Coaching collaborative writing is like training a team for a race. Writing and running athletes on a team

- Are put through the same exercises
- Execute the same workouts
- Create greater and stronger successes than they could accomplish individually
- Are afforded security so they can have the courage to put forth their best efforts
- Are offered opportunities to become leaders if they feel completely comfortable with themselves as athletes

The coach stands in front of the team viewing the strengths and weaknesses of everyone. The coach wants each individual to reach potential and to become a successful part of the whole. The title of "coach" works magically for children and sets a different tone from day-to-day teaching. Think of yourself as coaching students through to understanding—introducing them to organizing strategies and uniting their strengths to play toward a mutual goal. Play is a key element to the collaborative writing training session, from the competition of choosing a character in a series of vote-offs to having different children "own" lines as everyone rewrites together. Make collaborative writing fun from the very beginning by using "contest entry words" to introduce writing concepts. This sets up an environment in which children want to learn. Contests, like writing and marathons, have requirements.  Tell students that you're holding a contest and that they must do four things to win:

- They must find out what a given word means: "How would you find out what *conflict* means?" I ask to begin a discussion. Children discover that parents can be as valuable to them as a dictionary or thesaurus. Explain that you are off-limits as you don't want to choose favorites.
- They must put their name in the contest entry box (or anything else you have on hand for collecting their scraps of paper).
- They must get lucky—their name must be chosen.
- They must be prepared to tell what the word means if their name is chosen and explain it so the whole class can understand the definition. Rattling off a memorized definition doesn't count. Emphasize the importance of really knowing!

The contest entry words you select should be specific to the writing concepts you want to introduce, such as

- character
- motivation
- plot
- conflict
- resolution
- premise

Follow each contest with the reading of a picture book that illustrates that concept. If your minilesson is on character, for example, choose a book to read aloud that has a particularly strong character. More and more picture books are being written for older elementary school students. These provide wonderful lessons in a complete and powerful package. Books that invite questioning and discussion are best. An important part of learning to write is discovering what makes books work. During the literary discussion, you might discover more contest entry words that speak to stylistic elements of writing such as

- symbolism
- imagery
- metaphor
- irony
- allegory

You will want to introduce these because you'll ask that they appear in the individual writings during the write-a-thon. I used to save these lessons for a second draft, but then realized most images and metaphors tend to come along with the story. Perhaps they're strengthened later, but there are definitely word jewels embedded in the original creation.

## ▪▪▪ Play Meets Character

Always keep that sense of play going. "I'd like a volunteer from the studio audience," I call out and hands shoot up. Or I might request help from "my lovely assistant." Pretty soon the students are captivated by games and silliness and have forgotten their beliefs that writing is a serious business and that you *have* to learn it.

With banter and games, students are rapidly swept into getting to know the name, age, and family background of our new and intriguing group character. Then we're all spurred on to discover what our character looks and feels like, worries about, is motivated by. What problems does our character face? How does the character react or take action? Before we know it, a story emerges because the character is leading us from motivation to conflict and resolution.

As head coach, be mindful of your goal: you want to allow students to create a story that makes sense and has meaning for them. You want them to discover, through experience, a structure that will work for them in future writings. Your collaborative writing training

- Sets the stage, both technically and imaginatively.

- Carries the same information and routine as the write-a-thon, which will give your writing athletes the comfort of familiarity later on.

- Is crucial to the success of a write-a-thon. Students who are just dropped into the experience will be as lost and confused as a marathon runner who's only run sprints.

- Creates a shared experience from the lessons you've repeated again and again, the teaching that took you months to get across, and the breakthroughs you've discovered together.

- Sets a tone of excitement and fun that will change forever how your students view writing!

# Pep and Prep
## The Initial Planning of Your Write-a-thon

**CHAPTER 2**

Success in running and writing takes a plan. Part of the energy fueling writing and running athletes comes from building up excitement and successful strategies. This chapter will serve as a checklist to help you organize a month or two before your write-a-thon. Organizational goals that are crucial for writing or running success are

- Familiarity with the course to be run (i.e., a sense of what the two days will look like overall)

- Development of your support team

- Strategizing and energizing.

These three goals will be revisited with more specificity two weeks before the write-a-thon.

# Preparation Goal I: Setting the Structure

The prospect of beginning a marathon or write-a-thon can be intimidating. Maybe it's the writer in me, but when it doubt I make a list of the five *Ws: who, where, what, when,* and *why.* They apply to life as well as writing. When organizing a write-a-thon, these categories give the comfort of knowing you've covered all the details.

## What and Why

It's important to clearly define what a write-a-thon is and why you feel it is important to bring one into your classroom. Once you know the what and why, it will be easier to communicate that information to all "Who's" you involve—volunteers, parents, and any others. Here are some bits of information you might want to include:

- The write-a-thon will be two nearly uninterrupted days of student writing. During this time each child will develop a meaningful story from idea to a completed first manuscript. They will demonstrate in writing their understanding of character, motivation, conflict, plot, and resolution.

- A write-a-thon is a celebration of classroom writing and an opportunity for children to have the absorbing experience of professional writers that few children discover.

- A write-a-thon gives students extensive adult support of their writing. Most students need support to be courageous and to trust themselves enough to write meaningful stories.

- A write-a-thon allows children an immersion experience that their more typical divided days rarely allow.

- A write-a-thon shows children how much adults believe in the importance of their writing.

## ⊙ Who

The "who's" are those you want to contact and involve in the event. The write-a-thon's professional organization begins with gaining the permission of others involved in the lives of your classroom. These would include

- The administration. Begin by encouraging your principal to participate. That involvement will help the children see how their work has value to the entire school community.

- Art, music, drama, or other teachers who usually spend time with your students during the period you wish to allocate to the write-a-thon will need to be asked if your class might miss a session. Invite them to attend the write-a-thon if they wish.

- Parents or classroom volunteers should be contacted so they can give any necessary permission and be involved in all stages of planning (see specifics later in this chapter about ways to include them).

- Once permission is obtained, you will want to announce the write-a-thon in a school newsletter, both to build excitement and to announce volunteer possibilities for those who want to participate. Extend an invitation to other school staff to visit so that they can be infected with the excitement and add their expertise to the event.

- After permission is obtained, you might contact others who might have interest: school system officials, reading and writing teachers, local librarians, teachers from other schools, and even education professors and their students from any nearby university programs.

- Contacting the local press will allow the community an opportunity to see the kind of thoughtful teaching going on in its schools. At this point you might see if the press would like to cover the story and/or might be interested in publishing some of the stories written by the class. Both options are thrilling to the children.

**Where**

A classroom works fine. Students can sit either at desks or at tables. It might be fun to change the arrangement just to convey the message that the write-a-thon is something special. At the same time, you want familiarity so that the students feel comfortable. When I began coaching write-a-thons, I set up coaches' "aid stations" in desks that lined the periphery of the room. Later I discovered that when coaches sit at the table or desk grouping of their student athletes, they help writers stay on-task and their tracking gives the head coach a more informed perspective of the class's progress.

It's crucial to delineate an area for group coaching sessions away from the area set up for writing; space for students to gather on the floor for coaching sessions is perfect. Without this dedicated space, they may be so captured by their writing that you'll only get half their attention during your group coaching sessions.

You'll need a table removed from ongoing traffic for refreshments. This way you can avoid spills and distractions that keep writing athletes away from their work. Snacks, like marathoners' stops for water, should be periodic—not constant—events. If possible, set up coffee and a coaches' treat; it's a wonderful thing to nurture those who will be supporting your students.

 **When**

I recommend that write-a-thons take place in the late winter or early spring. You might want to coordinate your write-a-thon with one of the best-known marathons, the Boston Marathon, which has been run on the Patriot's Day holiday since 1897. In general, I conduct write-a-thons over two days, which usually works for school's and volunteers' schedules. You could also

- Schedule your write-a-thon on four consecutive mornings and have a special treat such as a game or other group activity in the afternoon.
- Add a third day for more leisurely pacing to allow children to be fresh, to complete their stories, and to leave time for sharing stories and celebrating. You may not need volunteer coaches for the third day.

Should you wish to take the write-a-thon into another phase by writing a second draft or adding a peer evaluation, wait at least one week. Professional writers give their manuscripts time to cool. Waiting allows write-a-thoners to enjoy their triumphs and rest up.

The write-a-thon as I have constructed it runs for two entire days. Children delight in having a long stretch of time to devote themselves to one process. Marathoners take periodic breaks from their running, and these breaks are also critical to the success of your write-a-thoners. They need periods of rest to maintain the level of intensity. Interruptions that seem critical are

- periodic breaks for moving (i.e., recess and physical education periods, which are the only outside classes I urge you not to cancel);

- snack periods, which in keeping the marathon theme we refer to as "water stations";

- lunch periods;

- group coaching sessions that serve as progress checks with coaches and athletes and make time for short lessons on upcoming writing issues.

All of these will be described in more detail later on.

## Preparation Goal 2: Rally Your Support Team

You can draft coaches from many places:

- parents within the school

- community volunteers who have an interest in children and your school

- student teachers from a nearby university

- high school students drafted from a writing class or club.

## ◉ Good Support-Team Qualities

The best way to ensure coaching success is to handpick volunteers you know work well in the classroom. Teachers and writers who have worked with children make the best candidates. The most successful coaches are usually people who

- can commit the time (while you can have people come for half days, I highly recommend that you attempt to get volunteers who can make a commitment for one full school day).
- enjoy writing.
- like working with children.
- are not timid about helping a child stay within limits or about pointing out a misdirection.
- are not afraid to problem solve with a child.
- are readers (for they very often have a sense of story and can help a child out of a writing difficulty).
- love seeing a creative process unfold.
- are not easily flustered.
- have a full command of at least the English language. It's also helpful if you can provide coaching in other languages if your classroom demands this.

## ◉ Enticing and Informing Volunteers

When you send home information, you want to be specific in requirements and expectations. Begin organizing by sending out a questionnaire and general information sheet (see Appendix 3). The information should begin with the whys and whats of the write-a-thon. At the coaching-the-coaches session a week or two before your write-a-thon, you will give more specific guidelines and instructions (see Chapter 3).

You want volunteers to know right away what their participation benefits will be. Student teachers and professors gain teaching experience. A high school honors student might turn the experience into a class assignment. For parents, the payoff will be less obvious. Many parents enter classrooms only when there is clear benefit to their child alone. For that reason, I include on my initial contact form some quotations from former parent coaches. Their testaments about the miracle of the event serve better than my words. As one parent said, "For me, and for most of the students, the experience was meaningful, demanding, and at the end gave a true feeling of the kind of special success that only comes after you've invested your mind, heart, and soul in a project."

## Preparation Goal 3: Pump Them Up

Once you've determined that a write-a-thon is possible and you have a sense of how many volunteers you have and what special treats you can deliver to your students, you begin preparing your athletes. At this point, you describe the situation and begin to build their excitement for the event. I equate this with the phase marathon runners pass through when they build up their mental strength for the task at hand. This is where your coaching relationship with them begins. Begin your initial coaching with

- a discussion of what a team is and how you've been a team during previous training.

- a discussion of team and individual sports (compare mind-set, training, goals, strengths, and weaknesses).

- a discussion of marathons. Your comparisons with the write-a-thon and a marathon might include

  ○ what happens in a marathon. (You might compare the twenty-six and one-quarter miles with something they're familiar with, such as the distance to a nearby town.)

◦ the traits needed to succeed in a marathon: endurance, determination, a desire to win, a love of running, and speed.

◦ the preparation necessary: training, lots of running, and support.

◦ what feelings one might have while running a marathon, such as frustration, anger, or disappointment.

◦ the support required for success, including healthy snacks, water, friends to cheer, and coaching.

At this point I approach the subject, asking for their input, uniting us as a team, and letting them explore the subjects in a general kind of way. At this generalized level, both you and your students will be amazed by the number of parallels between a marathon and a write-a-thon.

Athletes preparing to run a marathon are filled with questions about their capabilities and performance and the future. Questions are also the essence of good writing. Engendering an environment of speculation in either running or writing will

• build enthusiasm

• allow for personal, intellectual, and emotional growth

• enhance the kind of searching that fosters intrinsic learning

• model behaviors you want students to demonstrate when they write.

Coaches are acutely aware of timing. After you've let the suspense mount, announce your write-a-thon! Tell them

• when it will occur (what date and for how long).

• how you will prepare (see the next chapter for ideas).

• what your special coach and athlete relationship will be.

• about your support system. (There will be coaches to provide help at every step of the way. The head coach will always be there too.)

You should also announce the good and bad news:

- The bad news is that endurance and determination are needed to face the frustrations all athletes have.
- The good news is the privilege of being the only class in the school that is allowed to write for two whole days. There will also be other treats such as special foods, extra resting points as athletes need to take breaks frequently, and a celebration at the end of the event.

Open discussion should follow. Topics to cover might include

- what students need for support
- their concerns
- ideas for increasing the fun, drama, and excitement of the event.

## CHAPTER 3

# Get Ready!
## Structuring Support Systems

One of the most important preparations runners make for a marathon is establishing support systems. Recently a friend told me how her eighty-year-old aunt is still running marathons: "She started ten years ago at the surprising age of seventy and, because she wasn't all that quick a runner, she ran with physically challenged participants. Now at eighty, she finds that those she once supported are now supporting her!" As a writing coach, you know how difficult the task at hand will be for some of your students, but they are probably unaware of what they will be facing. So it becomes your task to build in lots of security systems for them to rely on while they press on to meet their challenges.

 **Get Ready, Writers**

You can ready your writers by building on the marathon image you've given them—support them with the stories of others who have gone before. This might be a departure point for a study of sports biographies. There are biographies for children of legendary or well-known runners like Mary Decker, Jesse Owens, or even the nine-year-old athlete featured in Julianna Fogel's *Wesley Paul, Marathon Runner* (Lippincott, 1979; grades three to five). See Appendix 2 for more ideas.

If you have never run a marathon, you might want to familiarize yourself with the process, gathering ideas and metaphors that you might use and learning stories of marathoners to tell your children. I found adult resources (also included in Appendix 2) full of stories to impress children. Several books recount the supposed beginning of marathons with a famous run by a Greek messenger named Pheidippides in 490 BC. He ran from the village of Marathon to Athens to tell the Athenians they had defeated the Persians. The story says that he gasped his news and then collapsed on the ground and died. Not only is this a great story to tell children, but it shows the importance of pacing during the writing process!

I coached one classroom that had two parents who had participated in a marathon. The husband had run the New York Marathon for three years, while his wife supported him from the sidelines. They were willing to come and share their experiences with the class, offering two different vantage points and telling stories that were wonderful metaphors help to set the stage for our write-a-thon.

The husband, also a writer, spoke of how he feared he'd never finish the race and was calmed by a friend who told him a metaphor about eating a watermelon. "It's impossible to think about eating a whole watermelon at once," he told them, "but it's possible to eat the whole thing if you just keep taking bite after bite." He spoke to the children about

- pacing
- finding their own writing rhythms
- how the marathon taught him things he never knew about the capabilities of his body and how the write-a-thon would teach them about the power of their minds
- how he gained the support of others running with him
- how important the water stations were to take a quick break from the race, which he compared to their breaks for recess and sessions with a coach
- how he "hit the wall" near the end of the race and thought he just couldn't go on but then found the resources within himself to continue.

He ended by telling them to have fun and showed his medals. Then his wife spoke about seeing twenty-two thousand runners begin on one bridge. She dashed about the city, catching glimpses of her husband as he ran through different neighborhoods. She remembered the transitions from one landscape to the next: the silence of the Hasidic neighborhoods, the high school band's loud songs of celebration, the deserted factories in Queens, and thousands of spectators on the Fifty-Ninth Street Bridge. I asked the children about the kind of landscapes through which they'd move. Because of their training, it was easy for them to see those landscapes as the creation of character, motivation, conflict, plot, setting, and resolution.

I read of one marathon coach who referred to a training schedule as having a map for your journey. One of the goals I hope to have accomplished in my training is for students to have internalized the map of the course through which they'll be traveling and to have a vision of the entire path they'd be writing. It is also crucial that they understand that

- We are all participating and supporting each other through this journey.

- Like runners, they may experience difficulties and joys in different places. Each bit of country through which they travel will hold different moods for them. They might feel exuberance at the beginning, the magic of finally seeing the story come together, the challenge of discovering conflict or continuing through fatigue.

- Everyone will accomplish the goal in a different way. I illustrate with stories like that of a New York Marathon runner who ran the entire distance backwards or a Vietnam vet with no legs who marathoned.

One year, I was fortunate in having a few children who had participated in a write-a-thon the year before. I was able to ask them to tell their classmates about how writing had been for them, what they'd learned, and what their strengths and weaknesses were. They spoke of how they felt exhausted at the end and had to keep going. They inspired their classmates by telling them of the incredible feeling they got from devoting themselves to an entire day of writing.

##  Gifts from Your Community

One of the pleasures of coaching a write-a-thon is seeing what kind of gifts of support come from your community. Your communications and the return of volunteer forms might yield unexpected and wondrous results. In one classroom, I discovered a parent who was an amazing visual artist and also enjoyed working with children in a collaborative process. Being a visual sort, she wanted to enrich the write-a-thon experience by creating, with the children, a whimsical map of the race course on which they could record and measure their individual and collective journeys. She thought one way to support children was with a visual measure of their distance gained.

She asked the teacher if she could use a bulletin board and then covered it with nine squares. Each one represented one mile of the terrain we'd be venturing through. She brought a folder filled with pictures she'd cut from a graphics catalog and asked the children to cut out pictures that suggested the landscapes through which they'd be traveling.

I was amazed at how happily and easily they set about the task of finding specific images that spoke to them of the conflict, characters, and/or resolution they'd find. We stapled these around our miles and then stood back to view the magnificence of our collaboration. We then named the miles. Again, I was surprised and pleased about the ease with which they accomplished this goal and came up with names that perfectly expressed write-a-thon pitfalls. The names they chose were:

Mile 1: Character Corner/Motivation Station

Mile 2: Conflict: Problem Pass

Mile 3: The Conflict Worsens: Devil's Bridge

Mile 4: Resolution: Resolution Rapids

Mile 5: Grabber First Sentence: Miracle Mile

Mile 6: Grabber First Paragraph: State of Setting

Mile 7: Don't Let Your Middle Sag: Conflict Cliffs

Mile 8: More Conflict: Trouble Torrents

Mile 9: The Final Resolution: Heartbreak Hill.

The last mile was named after the famous hill in the Boston Marathon that challenges athletes near the end of the race.

This volunteer also found a symbol for each coaching team. A lizard wrapped around a pencil, for example, became one token who moved the miles one group wrote. This provided a visual image for them to see progress. One team named their token Bob and all the writers put a "Bob" in their stories.

Moving the token gave some children the chance to take a break from their writing. Other children used the visual resource for inspiration. Several writers chose images from the map to become characters in their stories.

In another class, a man who'd marathoned in New York remembered the ritual of the athletes joining together for a prerace pasta dinner. As he walked back to his hotel, he noticed that the entire city of New York was celebrating with him by eating at the innumerable restaurants offering pasta specials. He decided eating pasta would be a great kick-off event for us—a way to celebrate the writers, show them support, and have fun all at the same time. He was right! The pasta potluck was a memorable part of the event for all the children. They probably enjoyed the food most, but my favorite part was when the pasta dinner's initiator gave a short tribute to the athletes.

In one classroom a parent provided a pizza lunch for the entire class. In another, one child brought in "pencil" cookies that she and her mother had baked. One mother who made dolls sent a reading/writing elf who became our class mascot. It's amazing how supported you feel from the outside, and I've always experienced a high percentage of parent involvement. I've also taken care to send notes of appreciation to each volunteer, being as specific as possible about the gift they'd given as coach, break supervisor, or goodie sender.

## The Return of the Volunteer Forms

When the volunteer forms have been returned, you will begin putting together your support teams. You will have to make some of the following decisions:

- How many children will each coach have?

- Will you use half-day coaches?
- Which coaches will work best with which children? How can you match interests and ability levels?
- How will you coordinate events?
- How will you coordinate the efforts of your support team?

During the first write-a-thon I led, students could choose any coach for help, though they tended to return each time to the same coach. This made a lot of sense as it was frustrating for children to have to tell their stories repeatedly, as well as hard for coaches to have to familiarize themselves with so many stories. Since then, I find that coaching teams provide better continuity for coaches and write-a-thoners.

Coaches who can be present during the whole process make the best choices and also have the opportunity to watch the write-a-thon unfold from beginning to end. If you have coaches who can only volunteer for one full day, then you might want to set up a team that will "pass the baton" so that the first coach informs the second coach about significant situations, stories, and strengths and weaknesses. Use half-day coaches as "floaters" if you have enough full-day coaches, but you can have set up teams of half-day coaches and it works fine. They might take time to hit their pacing, but soon they're all off and running.

## Supporting the Support Team

A week or so before the write-a-thon, I hold a Coaching-the-Coaches evening. As promised on the volunteer form, I make sure that there are refreshments and set a playful tone. My three goals are to

- excite the coaches about the event
- make sure my support team leaves with a sense of team spirit
- prepare the coaches to train our athletes.

Begin the event with an active exercise. Rather than tell the coaches about the principles the write-a-thon represents, show them. Give them a sense of the process the children will follow and have them write a little so that they feel a common bond with the athletes they'll be coaching. You could choose any writing exercise to loosen them up and build camaraderie, but I recommend choosing something that combines the elements you're using to construct your write-a-thon. Do something easy so that no one feels put on the spot or gets performance anxiety. You don't want to frighten off any of your coaches!

I like to begin by choosing a book to read, preferably one that inspires wondering and questions to give them a sense of the environment I want to create at our write-a-thon. I choose a book that would reach adults like Julius Lester's (1994) *The Man Who Knew Too Much: A Moral Tale from Balia of Zambia.* The story tells of a young mother who witnesses the miracle of an eagle calming her crying infant while she works in the field. When she finally tells her husband, he neither believes nor trusts her and follows her to work. She, angered by his lack of trust, is more determined to prove the miracle than share it. At the book's shocking end, the man, frightened by the eagle's potential harm, fires an arrow and kills his own child.

Story telling is a way to open people's hearts and minds, whatever their age. Reading aloud is an important part of both the write-a-thon and the writing process. After we've had a bit of discussion, I divide the whole group into small groups of two to five people (depending on how many attend the meeting). I've done this in various ways, either by dealing out cards and asking like numbers to find each other (this takes some time, but is kind of fun and really mixes up the group) or by letting people count off. I like to break up couples or friends who generally sit together at the meeting's beginning.

I lay out other books, similar in intensity, and ask that each group choose one to share together, either by reading aloud or silently. I don't fill them in on the stories, but let them discover the books together.

After they've finished reading, I ask them to collaborate on Coaches Playsheet I (Appendix 4). It's a lovely thing to hear groups of adults reading to each other and discussing the book's import. While they work, I walk around, joining in when it doesn't feel intrusive, helping to tell a story that's a bit long, answering any questions they might have. I don't provide a lot of time. I've discovered if adults have to work quickly, they don't self-censor as much, they work better as a group, and besides, I've promised them a short meeting.

When they've finished I ask them to stay in their groups. I tell them how easy it is for children to come up with characters. I show them the character idea file the children have written. I give them two minutes to come up with three to five characters. These characters are to be described in short phrases to give just a slight sense of character. I give examples like these, to help them out:

- an alien teacher
- a child who can't do homework
- a co-worker who's very strange
- a wolf who lives in the sea

I give them only a short time to finish, and then we make a collective list of all the characters they've invented. Next I ask each group to complete Coaches Playsheet II (Appendix 5).

Even the most reluctant seem to be captured by the story and feel encouraged to discuss character, and delight in the creative process. Initially, I was afraid that the exercise would fall flat, but I've sometimes found it difficult to move them on to the nitty-gritty description of the write-a-thon as many would prefer to discuss and create for a longer amount of time.

Finally, I ask them if they want me to make a character list based on their answers to share their work with their children or if they want to add the ideas to those their children have developed. Only now do I tell them that I had wanted them to

- follow an abbreviated course that their children have run before them and will follow during the write-a-thon
- understand the importance of the link between reading and writing
- experience themselves as writers linked to others who have written.

We next move on to more practical information. I go over the following list of principles and problems that might arise during a write-a-thon and give an overview of what will happen in the two days:

- The reasons for a Write-a-thon
  - A celebration of all class writing
  - A way to keep children on track with their stories
  - An opportunity for them to feel the thrill of victory.
- The coach and support systems
  - There is room for individuality. The write-a-thon is an evolving format, and they can find their own ways to coach (e.g., one coach used an image of getting a soccer ball to the net to explain conflicts; another went from one write-a-thoner to the next at his table and each knew when to expect a turn).
  - The head coach is always available for those who feel at all lost, confused, or have a question
  - There will breaks for recovery time.
- How the write-a-thon will be set up
  - Volunteers will be notified and reminded about their coaching times before the event. Co-coaches will be provided with phone numbers should they want to touch base.
  - A list of students on each coaching team will be given on the first morning. Ask coaches with any preferences to speak to you after the meeting. Coaches with special-needs students will be notified in advance. Check to see if any coaches want to have their own child in their group.
  - The detailed structure of the write-a-thon and coaching process will be provided. Be sure to supply a clear overview as well as specifics (Appendix 6).
  - Stress the importance of playing to our goals. Everyone should have fun.
  - Describe where students are now in the process of writing and developing writing skills.
  - Show how the room will be set up physically.

- Tell how the teams will be organized. I like to put the athletes' ID cards at their seats in the morning and team lists on the board.

- Detail how students will get their attention. My technique has students taking their ID cards and placing them in front of the coach without disrupting ongoing coaching. Newly presented cards go underneath.

- Describe the role of aid stations. At critical junctures, students will be required to check-in with their coaches. These points will be marked in the write-a-thoner's guide. Each coach will receive a guide (Appendix 7) of specific notes on coaching at each story point. They will initial each aid station on the write-a-thoner's guide when students pass it.

- The purpose and practice of breaks

  - Water stations are breaks for food or movement.

  - Group coaching sessions are meant to cheerlead, focus the children on the task at hand, support students in coming areas of concentration, and read the group a story, which becomes relaxation and a departure for a minilesson.


## ◎ Coaching Guidelines

I've found that there are some statements commonly heard from students that coaches can expect to hear. I list them here with some possible responses you may want to discuss with your coaches:

- "I'm finished and I'm bored." Each child has been told to bring a book to read while waiting, and they can draw story illustrations as well.

- "I need help!" Students will present their write-a-thoner ID cards and you'll work through them in order presented and as fast as you can. Warning: children are great at noticing when things seem unfair!

- "Can't you help me first? It's just a quick question." You may even ask if it's a long or short coaching need when athletes come to you. Then you might get permission from others to help that child first.

- "I can't." Giving an idea to inspire might help. Sometimes compassionate coaching works, such as "You're right, it is hard. Look at how much you've done!" or "I know you can do it! How can I help you?" You might want to identify this situation as hitting the wall.

- "I don't want to do this anymore." This statement comes from fatigue. You might be able to sympathize it away, but you might also help the child look seriously at the story and suggest a way that can encourage her or him back on course. Again, you might want to identify this as hitting the wall.

The following list of coaching tips is handed out, and if there's time you may want to talk these over.

- Coaches are looking for consistency in the writing. Characters should act in ways that make sense.

- Coaches are not afraid to step in and offer suggestions. Some students may have troubles, so don't be afraid to really coach them through to a story that works. You can inspire your athletes to greater heights with your thoughtfulness.

- When coaches feel over their heads, they should call for the head coach.

- When athletes hit the wall, coaches shouldn't be afraid to help out. If students need the coach to take over the physical job of writing, they should go ahead. Consistent thinking is what's most important. Keep letting students know they can do it!

- If one coach feels unable to get through to an athlete, another coach's style may work better. Remember, the write-a-thon should be fun.

- Coaches shouldn't let the writer solve a problem too easily.

- Coaches should make sure their writers are staying with their stories.

- If a write-a-thoner is wandering off into unnecessary complexities, the coach should push for a simpler plot.

- If coaches get a sense that a child can work more deeply, they should urge that child to do so. Press capable students for active verbs, images, and descriptions.

- Coaches should point out unbelievable or incomplete elements. Have writers state their reasons and allow only what they can defend.

# Get Set!
## Final Preparations

**CHAPTER 4**

As the day of the write-a-thon approaches, you, as head coach, should begin to coordinate final plans and to get your athletes ready to write.

## Volunteer Coordination

By now you should have received the completed volunteer forms and can determine how the write-a-thon will run. The forms will help you decide

- how many coaches you have and how many children each coach will help
- how many days the coaches can come and thus how to schedule and prepare coaching teams
- the appropriate coach-student matches (if you already know a coach's teaching style)
- the way to coordinate snack and rest breaks

Clear communication with the coaches can prevent slip-ups. Rather than long hours of phone communication and trusting to the uncertain memory of volunteers, I recommend written responses which clarify the plan, and gracefully remind your volunteers when they've committed to coming (see Appendix 8).

## Organizing to Solve Problems

Consider interpersonal styles when you match coaches and athletes. You may not know the style of your volunteer, of course, except for what's been written on the first form or from a brief meeting at the coaching-the-coaches night. But if you know some of your volunteers, you can make success more likely. For example, you may want to put a volunteer who you know to be wary of setting limits with children who are self-motivated. An authoritarian volunteer may have a difficult time with children who have difficulty controlling themselves.

At one write-a-thon, I observed a coach who had previously taught sixth, seventh, and eighth graders in a private school have a difficult time coaching a low-ability student. This coach pushed for excellence and greatly benefited the most capable write-a-thoners, but confused and was frustrated by those who struggled. He pushed his writing athletes on to a second draft, encouraging them to find more specific images, more active verbs and sparkling language. The adept thrived, but the lower-ability students stumbled.

Generally, ability grouping is not necessary at all. In fact, if your coaches don't request a certain level of student, it's best to give them a mix. This variety provides them with a spectrum of challenges to vary their coaching patterns. Warn coaches of special-needs students. I once saw a coach who was frustrated for an entire morning until he learned that one of his students could neither read nor write. Having this knowledge, he adjusted his coaching techniques and both were successful. Consult your Volunteer Form I (Appendix 3) to help you discover coaching preferences.

Sometimes I've had enough coaches to float around the classroom troubleshooting problems that arise and helping athletes who are hitting the wall. If there are not enough coaches to allow me to float, I coach the write-a-thoners who, for whatever reason, will need the most help.

If coaches are in abundance, I give preference to those who can work during the entire write-a-thon. This helps greatly with continuity. One parent said, "I had a really hard time coming in for just the second day. It felt like it took forever to familiarize myself with the stories. I wish the person who coached these kids the first day could have clued me in!" Thereafter, I have asked volunteers to phone the coach replacing them for updates on difficulties and storylines. This saves time and confusion and turns those second-day coaches into immediately effective help.

In a perfect world, the most successful coaching team would have

- a ratio of one two-day coach to four writing athletes
- one or two floating coaches to hand-hold students having a hard time, to take children out for supervised movement if needed, and to monitor and to help students who were ahead and wanted to move on to a further stage
- additional support teams to monitor breaks
- coaches who can work the full write-a-thon
- a head coach to float and monitor the overall situation

In addition to establishing your coaching structure, you also want to coordinate those who will help on breaks and/or bring snacks. Since it's easy to just send in a snack, you may receive too much food. Limit your snacks to three or four items a day and ask for healthy treats like carrots or popcorn. Save the volunteers who want to bake for the final celebration. Marathoners, if they eat at all, eat lightly. I'll never forget the insanity of one write-a-thon in which children grazed on sugar all day long!

## Preparing the Athletes

Every race has rules. I have three writing rules to help the children access their imaginations and escape the media images that are so present in their world.

- No violence. The blood and gore that so often dominate student writing provides easy answers that discourage true problem solving and can turn stories into cartoons.

- No stealing. Characters can't be copied from video games, movies, or television. Original characters lead to innovative stories.

- No disgusting or offensive writing. I use the example of the most dangerously disgusting story I ever wrote with children: *The Running Diaper*. Some children can become completely lost in the land of bodily functions.

I explain the first two rules to children by telling them that "I don't want to add to the violence in the world" and that "they can't use a character that someone else has already created because it's been done before." These rules also function to help students discover the creative scenery inside themselves.

I explain the third rule by telling the children that I want to write stories that will be read. A good measure, I recommend, is thinking how their parents would feel reading their story. "Writers," I tell them, "must be constantly aware of audience. It's just one of the writing realities."

I got into trouble the first time I put aside my "no stealing" rule. The playful ambiance of experimentation, excitement, and kid commitment dazzled me into reconsidering. Looking back, I realize I made an uninformed decision. One student asked if he could do a character from Mortal Combat. "They're not really real," he told me. Never having played the game, I made a wild assumption: how developed could a video game character be? It seemed like an interesting experiment for this child to make a one-dimensional character more real. I relented on my rule and right away five other students decided that they would pursue video game characters, too. They each picked different characters, and each had a grueling writing job ahead of them. They struggled for the entire two days, trying to make the characters their own. One other boy decided that he wanted to write a sequel to Star Wars and invent a new character. He ran into the same troubles, further proving to me the wisdom of following my original rule.

In my first write-a-thon, I had the class choose their characters the day before we began. Much of my decision was governed by a short amount of preparation time. Later, I reflected on how running athletes condition, stretch, and mentally prepare long before their marathons. As a writer, I dream about my characters for months before I ever begin committing them to computer screen. The imaginative phase of writing is an important part of the process. After that first write-a-thon, I made sure that my writing athletes really had that time to dream, imagine, and wonder about their characters. It's much easier to write with solid preparation.

We begin by pulling out a long character idea file we've composed together and reading aloud all the characters we created. I focus on a few, asking the students whether or not they think the character is strong, asking why or why not. "What's a stronger character: a bear, or a bear with magic powers?"

I tell them that runners prepare for races by testing their strength and building up their mileage and speed. Just as runners need strength, writers need a strong character to help them imagine.

I'm fond of sharing one story of character weakness that came during a collaborative writing adventure. We wrote a story about a boy who was born with tattoos. Dakota definitely began as a character who could make us wonder. We had great fun imagining all kinds of wild things about him—the kinds of tattoos he had, where they were on his body, and so on. After a while, I noticed that the children were dissatisfied and some were withdrawing. Finally, it took the tears of one child to really bring our character-building process to a grinding halt!

When we examined why the story wasn't working, we decided that we'd stopped caring about our character. We had so much fun designing wild tattoos and imaging silly things about how his tattoos happened that we'd forgotten to write about his heart and his mind and he became a weak character who held no appeal for us. I like to tell that story to children and to show them that we initially made the character strong, but didn't keep him strong enough to keep the wondering alive.

In further preparation for character selection, we discuss some of the characters they've previously invented or those in books and talk about what makes us wonder. I ask some children to talk about a character who's led them down a path of wondering. I then announce that night's homework: to come up with a character for the write-a-thon, a character who will inspire wonder.

The next morning we have a discussion about writing. "Some writers," I tell them, "like to keep a character close to them and not tell anyone until they've lived awhile with that character. It's similar to the way some people like to get to know other people. Some like to make friends slowly, watching and thinking before they really become close. Other writers, like me, find that when they talk about a character, the character becomes more real." I end by asking if anyone would like to share characters. Many do, and I love the oohs and ahhs of appreciation that their classmates utter.

I give homework for the following day too. I ask them to write at least five questions they have about their character, on the same piece of paper on which they've described their characters. "You can get help from home if you want. You can tell your mom, dad, brothers, sisters, or friends about your character and wonder together. Or you can wonder alone."

The next day, I ask them how many questions they've come up with and spend some time hearing about the one thing that makes them wonder the most. "You're going to have an opportunity to find out because tonight I want you to answer at least five of the questions you wondered about for homework."

For the fourth night's homework, I ask them to find out five more questions and answer them. If they groan, I ask them to pretend that they're starting a friendship with someone and to ask the kinds of questions they wonder most about a friend but can't always ask. Again, I urge them to talk to people outside of school, which builds their character as well as support, and enthusiasm.

For the fifth night's homework, I ask them to tell someone who hasn't been a resource yet just a little bit about the character. And I again push them to wonder more about this strong new character they're beginning to know.

## Last-Minute Athlete Coaching

Write-a-thoners need to know what to expect during the race. I begin by telling them that when people run a marathon, there's a big ritual when the runners pin their numbers to their backs. Our ritual will begin differently: they will find their name and identifying number on a desk. The desks will be arranged in writing teams. They will also learn who their coach will be in the morning. The write-a-thon ID tags will help the coaches learn the children's names and, when the writers need help, they can take off their ID tags and hand them to the coach.

Each write-a-thoner will also get a course map, called the write-a-thoner's guide (see Appendix 10), which will help them keep on the track. On the guide are directions that will lead them through our write-a-thon, beginning with defining a character and going all the way through to story resolution. Where students see "Aid Station" on the map, they will check in with their coach. If the coach thinks that they have mastered that part of the course, they can move on to the next part.

We will spend the first day planning the story and the second day writing a first draft. Remember that during a write-a-thon, the writers are not going to "race" but go slowly to give their stories all of their attention.

Homework for the night preceding the write-a-thon might include bringing:

- pencils, lined paper, crayons, and/or markers to illustrate the story while waiting for coaching time (use only pencil if you intend to reproduce the stories and illustrations for a class book)
- character notes developed from homework the previous week
- a book to read while waiting for coaching
- determination, courage, and a strong character
- a willingness to hear the coach, which means polite and careful listening and a cooperative spirit

A good night's sleep and a filling breakfast will also help.

## Details Make All the Difference: Last Minute Head-Coach's Checklist

Here is a miscellaneous checklist of those last-minute activities and things you might want to gather or check:

- Create a runner's tag with each athlete's "number" and names. These can also be used to get attention from the coaches and will help create a fun mood.

Scavenging in classroom closets will often yield supplies like stencils and markers so you don't have to buy them. Instead of pinning the numbers, hang them around the write-a-thoners' necks.

- Find plenty of extra pencils, markers, and paper (lined paper for writing and unlined for illustration).

- Copy a write-a-thoner's guide (see especially Appendix 10) for each child and coach. Don't forget to bring extra coaching notes for those who've forgotten them from the coaching-the-coaches night.

- Arrange coaches' and write-a-thoners' desks. Sometimes I've set coaches' desks a short distance away from the fray so children can get up and move periodically. Other times I've put a coach's chair right in the middle of a circle of desks to keep the children active, involved, and on-task. Both styles have their merits.

- Call the newspaper to announce the event, remind school staff who expressed interest in attending, and ask your principal to drop in.

- Choose the books you want to use to illustrate the group coaching based on the points you want to make.

- Set up a special table for coaches' treats (make sure there's coffee in the morning!).

- Prepare some kind of tribute at the end. I think that children like a symbol of their victories. I've enclosed a certificate that can be copied (Appendix 12). Medals can be bought or made too.

- Organize your outside support staff—make sure that there are treats for both the children and the coaches. Determine how you want to govern breaks.

- List your coaching groups on the board.

- Plan a complete schedule (see Appendix 9). You may not follow it exactly, but it will be a good guideline. Write the day's schedule on the board, including breaks.

- Send a note home to coaches to remind them to bring food and/or arrange for their lunches.

- Get a good night's sleep!

CHAPTER
5

# Go!
## *The Write-a-thon Begins*

 **Introducing Day One**

Begin the first day with introductions. First, introduce the coaches to the children by their coaching names, making personal connections when possible ("Coach Soandso is _____'s mom"). Both children and parents find pride in the acknowledgment and it helps your write-a-thoners feel joined to the coaches who will be helping them. Allow a short time for the children to introduce themselves to the coaches.

Next follows the introduction of write-a-thon rule 1: "Always listen to your coach!" In running and in writing, athletes may be so involved in their own processes that they can't see the whole picture. The coach has just the right distance to help them. I also want to make sure that all adults in the room are respected and acknowledged as authorities who are there to help.

I continually resort to storytelling as I lead the write-a-thon. I like to tell the story of one child who refused to listen to the coaches. She went through three coaches before she

came to me. She wouldn't listen to my coaching either, preferred to lose herself in her tangled story, and convinced herself that she alone knew what was right. I warned her that not taking the coaching seriously might jeopardize her writing success, but she was confident that she didn't need anyone's help. An hour from the end of the write-a-thon, she broke down in tears, fearful that she would not finish her story. At the time, all coaches were busy and couldn't help her.

Happily, during the home stretch, I found the time to help her out of her misery. Frankly, the time she'd had to sit pondering the consequences of her behavior strengthened her learning. For her and for other children, the write-a-thon often holds a larger lesson than in regard to writing alone. When I asked this writing athlete what she had learned from the experience, she was quick to tell me that she knew she hadn't listened to the coaching and that's what almost stopped her from completing her story.

She found pride in the fact that she was finally able to take coaching, though it was difficult for her. When she became insistent on doing it her own way, I stated that I would not spend my valuable coaching time trying to convince her that my suggestions were worth listening to as there were many who appreciated the time that I gave them. By the write-a-thon's conclusion, she deserved two gold medals—one for completing a successful first draft and a second for conquering her willful behavior.

At the day's start, I also announce who will be working with which coach. I will have written these lists on the board and the seating reflects the plan too. I tell the children that it will help them to work with one coach, though if their coach seems bogged down and they see another coach who has more free time, they might give their runner's number to someone else or ask a fellow write-a-thoner for help.

In brief, here's a checklist for your coaching introduction:

- introduce coaches and write-a-thoners

- announce write-a-thon rule 1: "Always listen to your coach!"

- assign writers to coaches, referring to the listing you've made on the board

 **Surveying the Day**

To bring a shared language to coaches and students and to invoke the spirit of playfulness, use marathon terminology:

- Restate the writing rules (See Chapter 4)
  - ° no violence
  - ° no stealing
  - ° no repulsiveness.

- Lay out the race course: how do marathoners find their way?
  - ° Runners develop a sense of timing, shown in your classroom by the schedule of breaks which has been posted on the board.
  - ° Runners follow maps. Each write-a-thoner receives a write-a-thon guide (see Appendix 10).

- Sign posts to show the way
  - ° Write-a-thoners should have the write-a-thoner's guide (Appendix 10) on their desks. Ask them to write their names on the guide as well as the brief character description generated during the training phase of the write-a-thon.
  - ° During a marathon there are aid stations that provide support in terms of water or medical need. Periodically, write-a-thoners will see on their Write-a-thoner's Guide "Go to the nearest Aid Station and talk with a coach!" At these points, they must check in and get story support and an initial from their coach to show they've completed this check-in.
  - ° How do write-a-thoners get support? In a marathon, runners are continually supported by a cheering crowd. Write-a-thoners can get support by presenting their runner's number to a coach. If the coach is busy, they can slip the number to the bottom of the pile, knowing they'll be helped as soon as possible. While waiting, they can do an illustration for their stories, reread their own work, or read a book they've brought.

# Road Hazards: Potential Writing Problems

- Keep your mind on pacing.
  - A write-a-thon is not a marathon: don't race! Take it slow and steady.
  - Don't worry about finishing; take things one step at a time. You can eat a whole watermelon just by eating bite after bite!
  - Find your own pacing. This is not a place to compete but to discover your personal best!
  - Runners and writers need a steady pace, immense stamina, and the ability to withstand temporary agonies. A winning frame of mind will help you withstand exhaustion and discouragement.

- Keep things basic.
  - Watch for too much complexity in a story and keep it simple. Runners get their race down to the basics. They don't carry a lot of extras with them.
  - Do not write about a cast of thousands. Focus on one character. Scattered thoughts are a roadblock to success.

- Keep your mind on such goals as form and style.
  - Athletes acknowledge the importance of having a goal and having the ability to adhere to a specific well-thought out plan to achieve this goal. The first day's goal is to develop the skeleton of the story by creating a writing plan. The second day's goal is to develop the style while writing—putting flesh on the story skeleton.
  - Marathoners often strategize by dividing up the large marathon goal into smaller goals. Prepare your students by reminding them of the smaller goals they'll accomplish: character development (both physical and emotional); character motivation; conflict; resolution.

 **Group Coaching**

No matter how small your room, designate an area for group coaching sessions. This can be a small area in front of the board (for a writing surface) so children can sit briefly to hear minilessons. I led one write-a-thon in a temporary classroom so small I decided not to set aside a special area. For the entire two days, I had to struggle to get attention during group coaching sessions. Eager students who wanted to get back to their own stories would scribble away, giving me only partial attention.

Group coaching sessions are short and to the point. They may include focusing techniques such as

- reading a book to lead to a discussion

- coach and writer check-ins

- a short lesson to introduce an upcoming writing session

Even if I am reading a book aloud, I still shoot for limiting these sessions to twenty minutes.

Spend a few minutes describing the group coaching session. I tell students that finding focus is crucial to both writing and running athletes. Before racing, some marathoners even meditate, visualize, or polish a skill in their mind's eye. I even read about one runner who chants to himself, "I'm a tough dude!"

At this point, check in with coaches and children. Ask the coaches if they would like to offer any advice. Then ask the athletes if they have any questions or comments they wish to make. Then move right along to the group coaching session on character development.

# Mile 1
## Character Development

**CHAPTER 6**

### Group Coaching on Character Development

As a writer, I believe all good stories begin with strong characters. To begin the first group coaching session, I read a book that has a strong character, like Ken Mochizuki's *Baseball Saved Us* (Lee and Low, 1993; grades four to six). The story involves Shorty, a young Japanese-American boy who is interred in a prisoner-of-war camp during World War II. During the story he fights prejudice and his own anger and discovers that channeling his anger into baseball brings him success.

When I've finished reading, we play the character game. I choose a "volunteer from the studio audience" who times us for one minute while we list as many traits as we can about Shorty. These traits can either be written on the board or added to previous lists of character traits you've prepared during write-a-thon training.

Having established a backdrop of character understanding and appreciation, I use the character we've discussed to introduce the next task at hand. I read some of the character questions that children will be answering on their write-a-thoner's guide and ask how they might answer them about Shorty. The form asks, for example, about obvious physical features and the children will easily be able to describe him as short and Japanese-American.

Then I pose another question they will have to infer. "What do you suppose might be three rules that Shorty's family has? It's obvious that he's supposed to respect his elders because his father is horrified by his brother's rudeness, but what do you think two other family rules might be?" Being imprisoned might suggest that he should follow camp rules, and another rule might be based on one of the story's premises, to refrain from judging people by what they look like.

End the session by telling coaches and students

- How long the next writing session will be (probably thirty to forty minutes at this stage).

- What will come after the writing session. (In this case, students and coaches will have a chance to move and snack.)

- Which areas they will focus on. (I usually list basic character facts, their character at home and in the world, character strengths and weaknesses, and the way their character feels inside).

- To really think about their character as they go, and not just answer questions.

- Remind them that they must check in with a coach at each aid station.

Ask if everyone has at least one sharpened pencil. Then we chant together "On your mark-Get set-Go!" Your write-a-thoners are off and writing.

## Student Writing

The early morning writing sessions are the most productive times of the day. There's also a strong tendency for some of your exuberant writing athletes to dash through the character questions with no concept of the character they're creating. In some cases this can't be helped as they are still trying to get a fix on their characters, but in other cases coaches can help their writing athletes right at the beginning by making sure that the questions answered make sense with the character they've begun to develop in their training.

## A Break!

After a stretch of serious writing time, it's time for a break. Some of your writers may want to skip the break and keep writing. This is not permissible! These break sessions are a valuable time for you to coach the coaches and to prepare a snack.

I tell children about the kinds of foods marathoners avoid. They avoid highly refined foods, sucrose, and saturated fats in favor of

- fresh fruit (e.g., fruit kabobs, orange slices, or apples with peanut butter)
- raw vegetables (carrots and celery in a cup whose bottom is covered with ranch dressing)
- carbohydrates (muffins, cracker sandwiches, rice crackers, or fruit cookies)
- health-food snacks

What should you drink? No, not Gatorade, or some other sports drink, but fruit juice and lots of water! Two easy ways to control snacks are to

- ask supporting food volunteers to provide healthy snacks
- limit the times to eat and the amounts of snacks that are supplied

While the students are shaking loose their energy on the playground or during physical education, you and your coaches can meet informally and prepare a snack that can be quickly consumed when the children return.

Two of the most important reasons for breaks are resting your coaches and checking in with them. Each check-in includes:

- asking how they are doing as coaches

- gathering comments about trends that can later be shared during a coaching session

- determining how far along each group is

- asking questions about difficulties with specific children

- discussing overall problems that need attention

- telling coaches of the next group coaching session plan

- requesting any insights, improvements, comments, or questions

Different phases of writing will also require different questions. During the session at the end of the first extended writing period it's important to

- See how coaches are doing with process at this first check-in; they may have a need to discuss and question specifics of the process now that they've seen it in action.

- Let coaches know at this point that their feedback is important. Their comments will help other coaches for this and future write-a-thons.

- Make sure the write-a-thoners are checking in.

- Evaluate whether writing athletes are understanding their characters or merely answering questions.

- Ask coaches what range of writing capability they are seeing and offer suggestions as to how best they can help their students. The goal is to help students write their best story. That might mean writing down the whole story told to you by a low-ability student or urging capable students to do their personal best. A coach's primary task is to help the writers succeed!

- Ask if any writers are creating "a cast of thousands." I once helped a young writer understand that there was no reason why her queen had to have six children. The queen became childless, and the story worked much better.

Before students return, coaches should place snacks on desks while you outline your next coaching session. A good percentage of the students will soon be moving from character development toward motivation, which will be the focus of the next group coaching session.

## Group Coaching on Motivation

I describe motivation in a story as "the thing a character wants more than anything." Very often motivation leads to conflict as the character has a problem getting what she or he wants. While write-a-thoners snack at their desks, I read another story that has a character with a strong motivation. Linda Altman's *Amelia's Road* (Lee and Low, 1994; grades three to five) is the story of a young Hispanic migrant worker who longs to stop traveling the roads and have a real home. I particularly like this book because at the story's end she doesn't really get what she wants, but she has found satisfaction.

After reading the story, gather your writers for a group coaching session. Speak of the motivations of the protagonists in both books we've read, then ask who knows what their own characters' motivations are. I hope weaker motivations come up in discussion. For example, someone might tell me that a character's motivation is to get money. I ask why and urge that they need money for food rather than a new video game because need is a stronger motivation than desire. A character could live without a video game, but not without food.

After discussing motivation, I call on each coach individually to ask for comments and coaching. A common coach comment at this point is that writers are just answering character questions without thinking. I like to give an example that's a bit silly; "For example, if my character is the Big Bad Wolf and I say that he's a vegetarian."

I ask students if they have any comments or questions. I then tell the writers that they will have another hour to continue developing their characters before we break for physical education or an extended morning break.

 **Break Two**

During the second break, ask the coaches about:

- how they themselves are doing
- trends that can later be shared during a coaching session
- how far along each group is. You would hope by this point they'd be nearing the end of character development and motivation
- difficulties with specific children
- overall problems that need attention
- any writers that are in trouble or need head coaching
- insights, improvements, comments, or questions

Specifically in this coach check-in, I also ask coaches about features of the writing:

- Are the characters beginning to develop?
- Is a consistent character emerging?
- Do you have a child struggling that could use one-to-one coaching with the head coach?
- Is motivation pulling the characterizations together?
- Does their newest character information make sense in terms of the character they've developed?

The next group coaching session will cover the character's conflict. I urge holding students back from writing about conflict until that session. Trying to prepare the coaches for upcoming writing issues, I suggest that they make sure the conflict is coming from the character that's been created instead of being pasted on. Some students may need help fitting conflict to motivation and character.

# CHAPTER 7

# Mile 2
## *Conflict*

As head coach, your goal is to get most of the students through the character phase before lunch. By then, they will have had at least three extended periods of writing. I'm always amazed at the silence, concentration, dedication, amount of completed work, and focus of the morning sessions. The afternoon energy drop always seems to come as a surprise as well, so it is important that a good bit of your work is completed before lunch.

 ## Conflict Coaching

I like to end the morning with a coaching session on conflict so that students come right back to work after lunch. From our training, they know conflict to be the problem in the story. Conflict is usually the driving force of the story, which I like to demonstrate by reading only half a story, leaving them in suspense. Also, knowing that likely there will be less work intensity in the afternoon, I shorten the periods of time that I read aloud. It is important to find

a book with a plot that has well-defined conflict that increases gradually in clear scenes and ends with a satisfying resolution in which the book's protagonist solves the problem.

One of my favorite read-alouds is David Shannon's *How Georgie Radbourn Saved Baseball* (Scholastic, 1994). It begins with Boss Swaggart, a baseball player in a slump, who plans to outlaw baseball forever and make everyone rich by starting factories. He gets his way and people are plunged into eternal winter because without baseball, spring doesn't come. Georgie Radbourn, a baseball natural, is born speaking only baseball terms. I stop reading at the point Georgie is arrested by the Factory Police when he is caught using illegal baseball sayings. There are generally groans and urges to keep reading. "It's the conflict!" I say. "It has you in its clutches."

We are then launched into a discussion of why conflict keeps the reader turning pages (you want to see how bad it gets and then how the problem will get solved). Students can look at the conflict in different ways. In part, the conflict starts when Boss Swaggart outlaws baseball, and if you look at conflict in terms of Georgie's character, the conflict begins when he has to work in the factory and is suddenly in sight of the Factory Police. In either case, it's easy to see that the conflict fits the story, which is something I want to see in the student stories—the conflict should fit with character and motivation.

I turn to the other stories we've read and we identify the conflict in each and discuss how it relates to the character's motivation. I use these stories to speak about how conflicts are generated. Conflict usually comes from a strong human need, like the need for acceptance (Shorty), home (Amelia), or freedom (Georgie). Being unable to meet those very human desires is a natural place for problems to begin.

Use stories to help the write-a-thoners make the following connections:

- Conflict must make sense with a specific character.

- Some of the strongest conflicts come when characters can't get what they want.

- Strong conflicts lead to strong stories.

I ask students who already know their story's initial conflict to raise their hands for some examples of conflicts. One writer decided that her nature-loving character would run away and then get lost. When she decided to add that her character gets AIDS, I wasn't really sure if that was to increase the drama of her story, please her father (who was her coach and an AIDS researcher), or to shock her classmates. Her first conflict (being lost) made sense with the character and her desires; the second (getting AIDS) actually took away from the sense of story. Young writers' wishes for complexity will frustrate them; they need to keep their stories simple.

When I listen to writers' examples of conflicts, I'm looking for rich sources of credible plot development such as conflicts that

- aren't going to resolve too easily

- can gradually grow worse

- have enough reality that given the context of the story—they seem plausible

When these elements of conflict development are missed, young writers tend to lose themselves in a writing maze before they know it.

During lunch coaches have a longer break to reflect on the morning's occurrences, to gather our wits, and to look both backwards and forwards. Looking backwards allows you to

- solve problems that have occurred (e.g. children who think they're almost finished but aren't)

- see which children need to be caught up

- discover what points of difficulty are coming up for writers

- have coaches communicate about which styles and solutions are working for them

Lunch tends to be a time to brainstorm about writing problems and to share strategies, frustrations, and coaching breakthroughs.

I remember a coach mentioning that one of his children had a Siamese twin character. The coach felt that the writer was only developing one character, and that one character didn't seem at all connected to his twin either literally or figuratively. Together the team of coaches came up with two options. One coach had just read an article about the amazing connections between Siamese twins and suggested she speak with the writer and share some of what she'd learned. We decided that if that plan didn't work because the writer might not be able to pull off this much sophistication, I would speak to him about focusing on one character and losing the twin. If the Siamese twin wasn't adding to the story, there was no reason to have one.

This midday break also seems a spontaneous time to share success stories. I remember one coach who struggled almost the entire morning with a child who didn't seem to be in sync with her character. Right before lunch came the triumphant moment when the coach saw the light come on in the student's eyes as suddenly her character became real to her and the story began to make sense. Being in the presence of the miracle of creation, especially when it occurs for less-capable students, is one of the most amazing elements of the write-a-thon.

Another coach struggled with a child over conflict. The conflict began when the main character had to follow strict rules at home. It took a coach to help the student realize that underneath all those surface problems was a deeper issue; his character felt that he had no power in the world. I remember the coach's amazement at how discussing conflict had led to a fourth grader considering the deeper meanings of life. The experience was even more incredible because the coach, knowing a bit about that child's home life, strongly suspected that the writer shared some of the feelings of his character. Watching a child work out life issues through story is a true write-a-thon gift and often what real writers do!

The lunch break is the best time to prepare for the rest of the day and devise ways of meeting your Day One goal of finishing a story plan. Looking ahead, you'll want to

- Lay out a rough sense of how the rest of the day will be spent
- Warn coaches that their writers will return with less energy.

This is an important time to coach about other problems that might arise in terms of writer temperament, for late afternoon is a time when write-a-thoners are more likely to hit the wall and pacing differences will show up. Some students will be finishing work and wanting to push ahead, while others are struggling to complete their work. I've developed solutions for some of these problems.

 **Hitting the Wall**

In marathoning, hitting the wall comes near the end of the race when the runner feels depleted. At a write-a-thon, hitting the wall can come in a number of different forms. The most typical is quite akin to what runners face: an exhausted, energy-depleted, and mind-numbing blankness. Some runners say it's the support of the crowd that gets them through this point. At a write-a-thon, a coach's support can be crucial. These strategies have worked in various situations:

- Take over the physical writing and let them talk out their planning while you write.
- Do an individual brainstorming session, giving them new ideas and perspectives.
- Ask another coach to step in who might have a fresh approach and ideas.
- Let them take a break—walking around the classroom, getting a drink of water, reading a little, or drawing an illustration.
- Let them talk about their story plan with another student who's finished to see if a peer can help them.
- Give them a sense of where they stand in the process. For instance, you may say, "you have only one more part to do and you have three hours to work in. I know you can do it!"
- Feed them one step at a time to counteract their feelings of being overwhelmed: "You work on one way that the problem gets worse and I'll keep your runner's number and come back to check on you."
- Tell a story of a marathoner hitting the wall, passing on descriptions and advice about what got them through.

For the latter case, I have included some of my favorite anecdotes about marathons and running:

- One marathoner describes his feeling of hitting the wall as his "eyes felt filled with sand and stomach full of writhing snakes."

- Another marathoner says he feels as if he's "trying to run through a brick wall."

- I like marathoner Grete Waitz's description of mental toughness: "to push when it hurts, fight for success, and dig down when you're empty and come up with more."

- Dennis Rainear ran the last sixteen miles of a marathon with a bullet in his head. He'd been shot but thought he had been struck by a rock.

- Many marathoners endure horrible diarrhea. This fact may even help a laugh to surface so your writing athlete can move on.

- Marathoners often keep going for the feeling of satisfaction and pride that awaits them when they can finally run the distance.

- Some marathoners break down the race to psych themselves: at six miles, they're one quarter done; at eight miles, one third done.

- Marathoners use many mental tools: the power of positive thinking, focusing on the event, deep concentration, eliminating outside distractions, and bolstering themselves by repeating statements like "Keep going" or "I'm a tough dude!"

These anecdotes might not work with more serious forms of hitting the wall. It's often time to remind athletes of choices and consequences when they declare "I don't want to do this anymore" or "You can't make me!" These problems are more serious. Before the write-a-thon, I arrange for an alternate place athletes can go if they feel this way and won't listen to coaching. I offer them the choice of going on to complete or leaving. Of course, they won't be able to participate in the victory celebration if they choose to go (I've never had a writing athlete choose to leave when these choices are presented).

You may even hear "I don't have to!" They're right. They don't. I make it clear that coaching time is precious, and I'm going to use it to help kids who want to write, not those who want to fight.

## Pacing Problems at the End of the Day

The end of each day is the time when you'll begin to see the biggest differences in pacing. This can create some difficult situations. At one write-a-thon, a child who could neither read nor write got a lot of individual attention and was one of the first to finish. He turned his subsequent boredom into fussing with someone else who had finished. One possibility for such low-ability students, especially those who like drawing, is to make a story board or a series of illustrations with a short description below each picture.

I created an especially awkward write-a-thon situation because I hadn't gotten consensus during a coaches' meeting. I decided that the children who had finished could leave to go outside, so that coaches could see who needed help. Unbeknownst to me, one coach had moved his athletes into writing a second draft. They were tired and wanted to quit on him when I announced my plan. If I'd only checked more fully beforehand, the situation never would have arisen. I remedied the problem with a public apology to him and his students, and told them that it was important that they finish their process. When they groaned, I reminded them to always listen to their coach.

Here are some strategies to consider to handle other pacing differences:

- Let the writers begin their homework (come up with a grabber first sentence and a grabber title).
- If they finish their homework, let them begin their next day's work.
- Have the writer share plans with a different coach.
- Have the writer share plans with a peer who has finished work.
- Let finished writers read or illustrate.
- Ask finished writers to help others who may be having a problem.
- Arrange for afternoon supervision, so that those who want to can go outside.

CHAPTER

**8**

# Mile 3
## *The Conflict Gets Worse*

In moving towards a goal, runners know the importance of consistent and continuous pacing. Young writers rarely have a sense of this. As a result, I often see either of the two scenarios surface in the second day of writing:

- Some writers become lost in one scene and then suddenly realize that writing time is coming to an end. They dash through the last several scenes in a short amount of time in order to finish.

- Other writers become lost in the writing and wander aimlessly through the story until it has no logical sequencing and loses meaning to both reader and writer.

Marathoners spend months developing a plan of action. Similarly, a story's plan of action is incredibly difficult for young writers. It's crucial, therefore, to spend time discussing how to plot the scenes of their story and then stressing the importance of sticking to that plan. The time you spend on plotting will definitely be reflected in the results you see on the second day.

Plotting is where the logic of a story becomes critical, and children often become

lost even while conceiving their plan. If they succeed in making a firm plan the first day, they can move more easily through conflict to their conclusion on the second day. Two actions you can take to help your writers are:

- devising a simple plan
- stressing the importance of definite scenes in your coaching sessions.

## The Story Plan

I've tinkered more with the plotting section of the write-a-thoner's guide than any other part. For example, I used to include character reaction and feelings with planning, but found that it was more helpful for write-a-thoners to make a straightforward plan that's composed of action after action. Think of this as the route marathoners run. If they jog off the planned path to discover a neighborhood or area of town that looks exciting, they might lose the focus and feeling of the entire race.

Story depth is dependent on the character's reactions and feelings, but many experiences have convinced me that those should be added during the actual story writing. When marathoners run,they are completely aware of surrounding neighborhoods, but having a plan firmly in mind keeps them on the route.

There are lots of different story patterns, of course, but one with clear sequencing has the strongest possibility of success. The plotting model we follow has children

- explore a character
- uncover what the character wants
- discover what problem the character faces (what conflict is occurring)
- build the conflict, making it grow worse and worse
- have the conflict climax when the problem gets as bad as the writer can imagine
- resolve the problem.

## ▊▊▊ Group Coaching on Plot

Begin the plot coaching session by returning to the book you're reading aloud and trace how the problem gets more difficult. Stop reading at the climax. This will anger your write-a-thoners. Tell them that the point in a story of supreme suspense is the climax and you want them to feel the power of it! Wonder together about

- how a good climax makes them feel
- how the author planned for the climax
- what unanswered questions they have
- what they think might happen.

In David Shannon's *How Georgie Radbourn Saved Baseball,* the problem begins when Georgie is born speaking only forbidden baseball terms. The plot unfolds in a clear path of problems. Each problem is represented in a different scene:

- First, Georgie goes to work in the factory and his parents wrap his face in bandages to protect him from speaking illegal baseball terms.
- Second, Georgie's mother's skirt gets caught in a machine and begins to pull her in, causing Georgie to utter a forbidden baseball term.
- Third, Georgie is surrounded by the Factory Police and put in prison.
- Fourth, Georgie goes to court, where Boss Swaggart has declared himself judge and jury.
- Fifth, Georgie can't stop using baseball terms and is finally gagged.

It's easy for children to find the problems. As they uncover them, I am strict about having them follow the order in which they've occurred. I like to write them on sentence strips so that I can move them around. Once we've found all the problems, we can look at what the author has done to create tension and suspense. What we discover (and I recommend you use a story that has a plot that exposes these kinds of elements) is that

- The problem starts out small and gradually and gets worse and worse. The conflict gets worse in stages in very separate events, or scenes.
- Each scene is built on the one before (switching the order of scenes doesn't make sense).
- Sometimes the problem seems to get solved, but then another problem comes along.

Sometimes I make a simple visual image of what is happening in the story. I draw a straight line, representing the path of motivation a character is traveling, and then cross this path with problems.

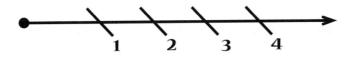

I draw the path of the problems, mounting the story line diagonally as it climbs to climax, allowing small places to plateau when there are temporary resolutions, stopping the line at the climax. For example, the plot of *How Georgie Radbourn Saved Baseball* might look like this:

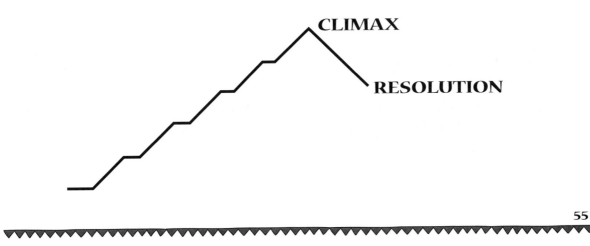

I tell the writers that being slow and careful in their plotting plan will help them enormously the following day. I tell them that good writers are mean writers; they get their characters in as much trouble as possible to build the conflict. If this bothers them, I tell them that writers make themselves feel better while they're doing this because they know they will come up with a resolution that's satisfying.

I show them the five questions they will be answering on their form:

1. How does the problem get worse?

2. How does it get worse again?

3. How does the problem get even worse?

4. How does the problem get even worse?

5. At the climax, or height, of the problem, how does your character take action?

I stress the following points:

- The questions are numbered to help them remember to let the problem begin in a small way and grow larger

- Every marathoner has a plan for running. This plan is the map of how they move through their stories during the next day's writing

- Just as a marathoner passes through different neighborhoods, *each* question should represent one scene the main character moves through.

 **Plot Coaching**

Coach your coaches about plot during the midday lunch check-in. Tell them that if they're demanding at this phase of plotting, it will make writing go more smoothly the second day. While plot coaching, they should be asking themselves and their write-a-thoners

- Does the problem fit with the story?
- Is the problem logical?
- Is the way the problem gets worse logical?
- Do the problems follow a natural progression?
- Do the problems fit with each other?
- Is the problem solved too easily?
- Is the problem too difficult to solve?
- Is the writer creating a plan with scenes that will be easy to write about?

You might tell the coaches that they will see a disparity in sophistication and will have to make a judgment as to whether a specific child can do better. For example, one fourth-grade student wrote a story in which her character was lost. First she met a bear, then she met an alligator, and so on, until she was found. While I would accept a worsening of plot like this from a child who has an extremely difficult time writing, I knew she could do better than this listing approach. I coached her to vary her problematic situations so that they would lead her to more writing growth. I suggested that perhaps when the night grew cold and her character had no shelter, she went looking for wood, then fell and hurt her arm. Once I suggested a specific example of how to vary her pattern, she happily improved her story.

CHAPTER

9

# Mile 4
## Resolution

Now that the writers have gotten their character into as much trouble as they can possibly imagine, it's time to get them out! One of the most difficult parts of this writing segment is that it comes at the end of the day. Having to muster enough brain power to wend one's way through to a logical conclusion is an feat for any writing athlete. Schedule a break before your final group coaching session. This will give you time for a last check-in with your coaches while your write-a-thoners get a well-deserved rest before the final push!

## Talking with the Coaches

This is a time for you to prepare yourselves for the day's end as you distribute healthy snacks. At this critical writing point you don't want to hinder your writers' ability in any way. This time should be used for both end-of-day and resolution coaching. Now, as the day's writing draws to a close, you want to find out

- who's on schedule and who's not
- who's in danger of not finishing
- who needs the help of the head coach
- what plan you will follow for the children who have finished
- if the coaches feel the writers have developed clear scenes that they will be able to write from on the next day
- if the stories are making sense.

## Group Coaching on Resolution

At resolution time, the old issue of violence often rears its ugly head again. I like to share with the writers the conclusion of the story about the boy who chose a Mortal Combat character. During my resolution coaching in his class, I asked for some examples of resolutions that the write-a-thoners had in mind.

The Mortal Combat writer raised his hand. "I'm gonna have my character out-whip the bad guy!" he told me.

"Anyone can out-whip a bad guy. That's easy," I told him, "The challenge for a writer is to figure out how your character can outwit, not out-whip!"

He, and the others who chose similar types of characters, continued their struggle right up to the end of the write-a-thon. When I asked who had the most difficult time at the end of the two days, I wasn't at all surprised at the hands I saw raised. These students were just as clear about the reason. "It's hard to write without violence!" one child told me, and his buddies nodded.

The coaching session about resolution is also the time to revisit a structure I've introduced in our training sessions. I remind the children about the three resolution "don'ts"

dying

dreaming

*deus ex machina* (This Latin phrase meaning *god out of the machine* refers to someone not previously introduced in the story who comes from nowhere to resolve the conflict)

These are common types of endings of children's stories. They are born of a frustration of not knowing how to end a story. I tell my young writers that every single one of these endings cheats the reader out of a real ending!

Only now do I finally finish reading aloud the book I began two group coaching sessions ago. I suggest you pick a book that shares the following elements with *How Georgie Radbourn Saved Baseball:*

- The hero of the story is responsible for solving the problem, preferably by taking action.

- The resolution comes in steps, in the same way that the conflict developed. This guideline steers your writers away from too abrupt, easily solved, or sudden endings.

- The story's end is a satisfying resolution (even if it's sad) that seems to balance the tension of the conflict.

- There's a great last line or comment that leaves a lasting impression.

In *How Georgie Radbourn Saved Baseball,* the resolution begins when Georgie offers Boss a baseball challenge. In other words, when he's as stuck as you can imagine, and gagged in the courtroom, he takes action. The end of the story proceeds in stages:

- Boss accepts the challenge, and the author builds up the resolving climax in a series of three strikes (one is even a hit, but it goes foul). The resolution is solved in steps.

- At the last strike, the readers are ready to cheer with Georgie. In fact, one of the times I used this book during a write-a-thon, a coach with a wonderful sense of drama read the resolution and had the class cheer as if they were the crowd!

- The resolution brings the story full circle when spring comes again. This is a wonderful writer's technique called "putting the snake's tail in its mouth"—or creating a sense of the story having come full circle for a satisfying conclusion.
- Shannon ends his book with a visual joke: "And there are still jobs to do, only now, some of them are at the ball park." And Shannon, who also illustrates the book, gives us a final picture of Boss Swaggart fallen from power and selling peanuts!

I then take the write-a-thoners through my don't checklist, with a series of questions:

- Would you have felt cheated if Georgie was gagged in court and then suddenly keeled over dead?
- Would you have felt cheated if the story had this great conclusion and then ended by saying, "And then Georgie woke up. It was all just a dream."?
- Would you have felt cheated if Georgie was in a tough spot in pitching to Boss and suddenly Superman swooped down and became a substitute pitcher?

The answer to all these questions is always a resounding yes. And then I ask my final question: "Who solves the problem in the story?" "Georgie!" they shout. We then discuss why this is the best ending. If time isn't too short, I ask some writers what they imagine their resolutions might be.

## Writing a Grabber First Sentence

Before I dismiss them to their final writing session of the day, I announce the homework. "Come in tomorrow with a grabber title for your story and a grabber first sentence. Both of them should really hook your readers!" I coach a bit about the "grabber first sentence." In one write-a-thon we labeled this step the "Miracle Mile" because it seems to be one of the easiest parts of the whole process. There are a few criteria/stipulations:

- The first line has to relate to your story. You can't just use a shocking sentence that has no meaning to the rest of your story.

- The first line should be a good introduction.

- The first line is how you'll lead into your action.

It's the end of the day, and the athletes are tired, but quickly mention the tone of the next day, as their homework will help frame the next day's work. Coaching should include

- the importance of using words to set the story's tones (describe elements you've talked about in training: images, senses, metaphor, simile, active verbs)

- the possibility that a race can turn out differently than an athlete imagined.

Set the mood by sharing a few book beginnings to give examples of differing story starts. Some good examples are:

- Drama: "The loud boom of drums frightened Prince Rakoto." (*The New King* by Doreen Rappaport, Dial, 1995).

- Strong emotional tone enhanced by description: "It had just begun to snow when a bent little man limped up our front path, carrying a tattered cardboard box wound around and around with twine." (*The Tie Man's Miracle* by Steven Schnur, Morrow, 1995).

- Setting through words and tone: "Naupa pacha, once upon a time, in the great city of Cuzco, in the ancient Inca kingdom of Peru, a prince was born to the Sun King." (*Miro in the Kingdom of the Sun* by Jane Kurtz, Houghton Mifflin, 1996).

- An immediate problem: "Long ago, in the time of shackles and slavery, there lived an enslaved man called Hezekiah." (*Foot Warmer and the Crow* by Evelyn Coleman, Simon and Schuster, 1994).

- An eccentric character: "Gritch the Witch woke up grouchy, grumpy, and very hungry." (*Piggie Pie* by Margie Palatini, Clarion, 1995).

- An air of mystery: "As it turned out, Grandmother was a far more mysterious woman than any of us knew." (*Grandmother's Pigeon* by Louise Erdrich, Hyperion, 1996).

- Humor: "The Princess kissed the frog. He turned into a prince. And they lived happily ever after. . . . Well, let's just say they lived sort of happily for a long time. Okay, so they weren't so happy. In fact they were miserable." (*The Frog Prince Continued* by Jon Scieszka, Viking, 1991).

The amount of teaching you can do will depend on the time (and level of fatigue). You may want to present these grabber sentences in your kick-off coaching in the morning. On occasion, I've merely read some openers to set a thoughtful tone and then left discussion for the following day.

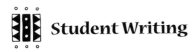 ## Student Writing

During this last session, you will see a huge range of problems and emotions:

- Some writing athletes will be hitting the wall.

- Others will be finished. Some will be bored and looking to disturb those finishing. Others will be chomping at the bit to get on with writing their stories.

- Others will have painted their characters into such a corner, they'll need your help with the resolution.

Stay aware of how your coaches are doing. I've seen situations in which some coaches are finished with their own athletes and can devote themselves to helping other groups.

 **Wrapping It Up**

As the day draws to a close, remember the following points:

- Remind the write-a-thoners of their homework.

- Ask them to get a good night's sleep.

- Find out which writers have not finished their plans. Reassure these writers that they will finish, and make a date with them for the first thing the following morning.

- If there's time, ask what they learned, what was hardest, what they enjoyed the most, and if they had fun. An important part of the write-a-thon is inviting them to examine their own creative  processes. If you run out of time, you can ask these questions the following day.

CHAPTER

# 10

# *Mile 5*

## *The Grabber First Sentence*

 **Introducing Day Two**

The second day of writing is very different from the first, and these differences merit a long coaching session. The first coaching session that day should tackle these four important issues:

- the difference between planning a story and writing a first draft
- grabber first sentences
- setting the tone for style
- grabber first paragraphs.

Begin the new day with an introduction, describing again the course they will travel. You should include

- An introduction of new coaches (those present and any half-day coaches who will arrive later in the day).

- Announce breaks from the schedule which you have already posted on the board.
- Announce the writing journey you'll travel with a brief description of each mile. These should be as follows;
  - Mile 5: The grabber first sentence (discussion of homework)
  - Mile 6: The grabber first paragraph (the whos, wheres, whats, whens, and whys of stories)
  - Mile 7: The middle miles (getting the story going, the beginning scenes)
  - Mile 8: The home stretch (building the conflict and climax)
  - Mile 9: Resolution (resolving your story's conflict)

## Crank It Up!

When marathoners go up hills, they have to work harder to maintain their pacing. Writing the first draft can sometimes feel like running uphill, and your writing athletes will need a great deal of endurance, determination, and strength to finish their first drafts. Prepare them for the shift, but also pause to admire how far you've come already. If you haven't had time the day before to examine the writing process, this is a good point to ask some questions about their difficulties, triumphs, and writing discoveries.

Move on quickly to discussing how the second day's writing goals are different from those of the first day. Name specific requirements of the first draft to make the goal more clear. As with the planning phase, first drafts are idea driven, but there are two differences:

- Though everyone will be following the same course, they will move through it in different ways and at different speeds.
- The coaching will focus on ideas and on the way those ideas are expressed. On the second day coaches may support writers in discovering words and images to make the story more powerful and clear.

There are important things the writing athletes can do to help their coaches:

- Remember write-a-thon rule I and listen to the coach.

- Skip lines while writing so work can be easily read and there's room to add ideas or words.

- Check in with a coach when the write-a-thoner's guide notes an aid station and whenever in doubt.

- Advise writers to look at what's expected as shown on the evaluation lists on their guide. They should do this before they begin writing so that they'll know what's ahead. Draw attention to the introduction of stylistic elements. I like to read one checklist aloud.

## Group Coaching on the Grabber First Sentence

Begin mile 5 by reading a book. Select just one book for the entire day because you can follow the path of one story and take more time to examine the elements, as writers are examining their own writing strategies and skills. This means the book needs to have all the qualities you will be looking for throughout the day:

- a grabber first line

- a grabber first paragraph

- strong characters

- the continual use of powerful images

- clear scenes

- a satisfying resolution

- an emotional component of some kind that will leave an impression.

One of the strongest books I've shared in classrooms is Patricia Polacco's *Pink and Say* (Philomel, 1994; grades four and up). I especially like this book for write-a-thons because it is a long picture book that's easy to divide into reading sections and it inspires strong literary discussions. It's sophisticated, so it needs an audience mature enough to understand both emotional, stylistic, and historical elements.

The author tells the true story of her great-great-great-grandfather Say, who was a young white Civil War soldier. Say was rescued from the battlefield by a young black soldier named Pinkus Aylee, who later perished at the Confederacy's Andersonville Prison. Say spent his life telling the story because he felt that Pink, a more worthy young man than he, had no birth or death certificates, and no family to remember him. Say was the only person on earth who could testify to Pink's existence. I begin my first coaching session by reading the first two lines of *Pink and Say:* "I watched the sun edge toward the center of the sky above me. I was hurt real bad."

I then ask what those two short lines tell us and include some or all of the following points in discussion:

- The story is told in first person. You can discuss advantages of third and first person. First person makes it easier to crawl into someone else's skin, but you can only see through that person's eyes. You have a wider view in third person, but it's sometimes harder to get the reader engaged.
- The character has a big problem and we wonder why.
- The character is lying on his back, giving some sense of setting.
- The author opens with a strong visual image.
- The book has a poetic beginning.

Ask the write-a-thoners to share some of the first lines they've done for homework. Discuss their work, using it to teach, excite, and affirm. In each example, point to the way they make the reader want to read more and how they make the reader wonder. Here are some examples of great first lines write-a-thoners have created and their strengths:

- "The one thing in the world that David Smith, also known as Wheelchair, wanted was to be the same as everyone else." (Getting character, motivation, and a hint of problem out quickly.)

- "Merk loved being chubby because it protected him until he met Meat." (A great revealing of two characters and their conflict.)

- "Dad had hired a very mysterious, spooky babysitter for his twin daughters, Lauren and Laurie." (I know this is going to be a story of suspense.)

- "My hair is blue and my heart is too." (This grabber first sentence promises a lot of poetry and beautiful images.)

- "Once, in Vegetable Land, Mr. Celery and his friends were having a delicious dinner of dirt sandwiches at Mrs. Tomato's house." (Humor or what?!)

- "Max and Pablo had been friends almost their whole lives, at least that's what Max thought." (Conflict between friends is an especially intriguing beginning.)

- "A crowd of skaters was circling the rink and all turned at once when Angela floated among them." (I wonder if this talented skater is hated or admired by the crowd?)

- "'I'll bet my castle, my animals, my servants, and even my wife,' declared the King of Gibralter." (Conflict through dialogue.)

# CHAPTER
# 11

# Mile 6
## *The Grabber First Paragraphs*

### ▓ Group Coaching on Setting Continues

Shift gears and begin preparing for the day ahead. Read just a page or two of a book, with the intention of examining setting. Use a book that gives a strong sense of setting in the beginning pages by letting readers know the who, what, where, when, and why.

*Pink and Say* supplies many facts and emotions on the first page. Because there is much to teach in this first coaching session, I read only the first page, which tells of a badly wounded boy who dreams of home. Begin discussion by asking writers to locate on this page the

> who (a young soldier)
>
> where (far from home)
>
> what (he's been wounded)
>
> when (Civil War)
>
> why (he's alone and missing home)

In order to attend to different styles of learning, discuss how the illustrations add to the story. In interviewing Polacco, I learned she grew up with severe learning disabilities and kept these hidden until high school. No one knew that she had trouble reading, writing, and doing math for all those years. She could draw well from an early age and so illustration is an important part of her artistic expression.

 **Group Coaching on Style**

Your next discussions will set the tone for the day, so it's worth spending some time analyzing how the story works in terms of style. Perhaps your writers won't be able to mimic this high level of artistry, but discussing style will reintroduce elements that you have covered in training. Presenting them again will increase the odds of being able to ask writers to demonstrate these elements in their stories. You might include

- "Show not tell." One of the first things fiction writers need to learn is how to let readers know about character and setting through action. We know the soldier misses his Ohio farm when he dreams of his mother's homemade biscuits, Polacco is telling us the soldier was scared, lonely, and missed his home. She lets us know much more by not saying these things and showing them to us. Showing is a way of respecting readers, and leaving them room to think and wonder. Spend a bit of time listing all you know about the story and character by what Polacco shows on the very first page.

- Voice. It matters how you tell a story.
  - Ask what you know about the character from the way he talks (he's not well educated in school but his senses sure are developed!).
  - How does the voice set the mood for the story? *Pink and Say* is full of drama, feeling, and a sense of history.

- Using the senses.

- Reread the first page and have students raise their hands when they hear Polacco using her senses.
- Using more senses makes a story richer. How many does she use on just the first page (feeling, hearing, seeing, and tasting).
- What's the difference between saying a character has been wounded and "my leg burned and was angry"?
- Imagery. Give a brief lesson on metaphor and similies.
- Word choices. Words matter, so make them count. Choose verbs that have action. I suggest selecting adjectives and adverbs only when you need them (many young writers get hung up on trying to sound like "writers"). For those times when you know you don't have the right word, leave a blank and come back to it later.
- Wondering. Good writers keep their readers involved by making them wonder.
  - Polacco makes you wonder by leaving you with a cliff hanger (you have to turn the page to see who belongs to the "strong hands" and what he'll do).She tells enough about the wounded boy to make you care about him and want to know more, but doesn't give everything away all at once.
  - What are the questions you wonder about and that make you want to turn the page? For instance, who's the new character? Will he help or hurt?

## The First Few Paragraphs

Now comes the time for your writers to apply what they've learned from your reading. The write-a-thoner's guide has evaluations that will help writers remember the lessons you've just taught, for you want these elements to appear throughout the story. Keep play alive by issuing challenges. For example, Challenge 1 asks your young writers to satisfy everything in the First Paragraph Evaluation (see First Paragraph Evaluation in Appendix 10, page 133) in their write-a-thoner's guide. It includes, among other things, who, where, what, vivid verbs, and descriptions.

*Challenge 1: Can you satisfy everything in the first paragraphs evaluation?*

**First Paragraphs Evaluation**

_____ I can tell when this story takes place.

_____ I can tell where this story takes place.

_____ I can tell who this story is about.

_____ This story makes sense to me.

_____ The writer has let me know how the main character feels.

_____ I'm pretty sure I know the problem in the story.

_____ The writer used at least one metaphor or simile.

_____ The writer used at least one description that used the senses.

_____ The writer used vivid verbs.

Then suggest *Challenge 2: Can you show without telling? Here are some examples to inspire and instruct:*

- Play with getting the time across without just telling the date. A character could read a newspaper, drive a "new" car that hasn't been made in years, or hasn't been made yet, or be raking leaves to show a fall setting.

- Instead of saying a character is a glutton, have him or her wander to the refrigerator and pig out several times in the first few paragraphs.

- Demonstrate feelings through actions. An angry character stubs a toe by kicking a table, while a joyous character hugs a younger sibling. Use evocative verbs: someone crabby might growl like a dog, and someone who's excited might chirp.

*Challenge 3: Remember to skip those lines!*

After issuing your challenges, send your write-a-thoners off to work before they take their first break. Ask them to begin by writing their names and grabber titles at the top of their lined paper.

As head coach, you might want to spend this first session helping the write-a-thoners who did not have time to finish yesterday's story plan to catch up before they feel like they're left in the dust!

## The First Coaching Check-In

While the write-a-thoners are having a break after the first writing session, check in with your coaches . Ask them the following questions:

- Do they have any students who have not finished their story plans?
- Have those that didn't finish yesterday caught up?
- Are there any writers who are having problems transitioning from planning to writing? How have they, as coaches, been able to help?
- Are there any writers who need the support of the head coach?
- Are they having difficulty getting the who, what, where, when, and why into the initial paragraphs?
- Are writers able to include some elements of style in their paragraphs or is much coaching needed to help with this? Are there any areas that need to be addressed in the upcoming coaching session?

- Have any writers successfully met the three challenges? You might want to mention these students and teach from their work at the next coaching session.

- Are all the students checking in? Are the coaches remembering to go through and sign off the evaluation checklist?

- Are there excessive numbers of invented spellings? When you read through a manuscript at check-in, write correct spellings. This will help coaches who see this child's story later.

- Are the writers skipping lines?

After you have evaluated the current writing environment, it's time to prepare the coaches for Mile 7, the middle miles. This is a writing session in which

- Coaches will begin to see a wide range of writing skills. Some students may write several paragraphs while others will write several pages.

- Write-a-thoners are supposed to check in at the end of every scene, though many may neglect to do so.

- Some students may have a difficult time with pacing during the middle miles. Some examples of pacing problems are

  ○ Being mired in minutiae. Picture the student who describes everything in minute details. The family going on vacation packs, gets in the taxi, travels to the airport, waits in the ticket line, and on and on with pages of description without movement. This kind of writer often ends up cramming the major scenes of the story into one paragraph because so much time has been lost in detailing.

  ○ Missing the middle. Here, a writer opens up with a strong scene and ends with a strong scene, but has little or nothing in between.

  ○ Developing scenes that go nowhere. Every scene should have a reason for being.

○ Forgetting the plan. While stories do change as they grow, this is the writing stage where some students completely forget the scene plan they developed the previous day and wind up in a tangle. In this short amount of time, their best bet is sticking to their plan!

Finally, remember to collect comments and suggestions from the coaches and head right on to face the middle miles!

# Mile 7
## *The Middle Miles*

C H A P T E R
# 12

## Group Coaching on the Middle Miles

While write-a-thoners snack and regroup, begin the coaching session congratulating those who met all three challenges. Read some of the work of those who want to share. Then move directly into coaching the middle miles by reading aloud the middle of a book, stopping before you reach the book's climax. Go back and have the writers name the scenes. How does each scene move the story along? Consider *Pink and Say*.

> Scene 1: The story is set as Say lies wounded on the battlefield. This reveals Say's character and sets up an intial conflict and tone.
>
> Scene 2: Pink and Say meet. This scene develops the relationship between characters.
>
> Scene 3: Pink carries Say home. This scene reveals Pink's character, and serves as a transition to get characters from one place to another.

Scene 4: We meet Moe Moe Bay, Pink's mother. We begin to care about her as a character, and learn more about Pink and Say's motivations and conflicts. Pink wants to return to fight the war against his mother's wishes, but Say feels he's a deserter.

Several transition scenes occur: Not much "happens" on the plot level but we learn more of Pink and Say's inner feelings, motivations, fears, and conflicts. The conflict about leaving grows.

Looking closely at these scenes serves to

- demonstrate how many different kinds of scenes there can be in a book
- show how every scene moves the book along
- explain how the scenes build on and grow out of each other.

Before releasing your write-a-thoners for an extended writing period, offer these words of coaching wisdom:

- If your scene doesn't add anything to your story, get rid of it.
- Stick to the scenes you planned on day one.
- Writers don't tell everything they know. Pick the really important details and ideas that move the story along in some way. Don't spend forever on one scene; once a point has been made, move on! You're going to have to keep the pace steady to cover every scene.
- Don't waste time when you write dialogue. If someone sits down next to a person he doesn't know on the bus, cut to important conversation. Don't waste time in unnecessary exhanges such as

    "Hi, how are you?"

    "Fine, how are you?"

    "What's your name?"

    "What's yours?"

Characters should speak to show they have a reason for talking, whether it's connecting with other characters or revealing some aspect of themselves. For example,

"Today was the worst day of my life."

"What happened?"

"I got the worst bully in the school mad and now he's gonna get me!"

- Writers should check in with their coach, especially after they finish a scene and whenever they're unsure about their story!
- Skipping lines is still important.

To meet the middle miles evaluation challenge, writers must include elements such as: clear presentation of problem, character reaction, and logical conflict development (see Middle Miles Evaluation, Appendix 10, page 133).

Let students write for an hour or so before they go off for physical education or an extended period of movement.

# Mile 8

## *The Home Stretch—Tension Builds to a Climax*

 **Getting Ready for the Home Stretch**

As writers experience the joy of a longer period of movement, the coaches can relax a bit and prepare themselves for the home stretch. During this writing session you face the possibility of writing athletes hitting the wall. It might help to review (and tell second-day coaches) strategies to help students facing writing exhaustion (see p. 49).

The stories should conclude with a strong climax. Coaches should make sure that

- this is the highest dramatic place in the story
- the climax makes sense in terms of the scenes that have gone before
- the ascent to the climax is steady and doesn't come out of nowhere
- the climax has a this-is-as-bad-as-it-can-get quality
- the climax might be something that changes the character forever

At this point, you should begin to prepare coaches for the conclusion of the write-a-thon by

- Reminding them to collect grabber titles so that during a working lunch you can fill in certificates with the authors names' and titles of their stories (see Appendix 12).
- Finding writers who seem to be in jeopardy of not finishing their stories, and asking about who needs help from the head coach.
- Reminding coaches that if they get stuck with a student, they can call in another coach with fresh vision who might reveal something previously hidden from a writer and coach or whose new approach might work better to get a child unstuck.
- Persuading students who are stuck to go back to their plans.

## Group Coaching on the Home Stretch

Read the "home stretch" of the story. *Pink and Say* moves through the following scenes:

- The shooting of Moe Moe Bay
- The boys' journey to find their units
- The boys' capture
- The climax, when the boys are taken to Andersonville Prison.

Have the group discuss

- How Polacco builds the tension to a crescendo at the climax with mounting dramatic events. The scenes before were important to the story, but they didn't carry the same impact.
- The relationship between the emotions and the actions of the characters.
- How one dramatic event leads to the next.

- How Polacco builds these scenes on each other, with the horrors of war growing increasingly worse.
- How it feels to have to sit with the climax, not knowing the ending of the story.

Offer these wise coaching words before releasing your writers:

- Make sure that the way the problem gets worse makes sense.
- Watch pacing; don't build too slowly (this can put a reader to sleep) or too quickly (give the reader time to care).
- Make sure the character has a reaction in emotion or action. A character might solve the problem only to have a related issue come up.
- Don't make the problem ridiculous.
- At the climax, the story should be as intense as can be imagined.
- Style can help. Sometimes writers increase drama with superactive verbs and quick, short sentences.

Can you meet the home stretch challenge? The Home Stretch Evaluation (Appendix 10, page 133) makes sure the problems and reactions are believable and the climax is strong. The writers have one more short writing session before lunch.

CHAPTER

# 14

# *Mile 9*
## *Resolution and Celebration*

## Preparing for the Day's End

Once again, lunch is the last long break coaches have to rally before the end of the write-a-thon. Generally, this is a working lunch to let coaches fill in completion certificates while they evaluate progress and problem solve. During this busy midday break you should

- Check on general progress and pinpoint those who will need extra help to either catch up and those who have finished early and will need to find new focus as the write-a-thon concludes.

- Go over resolution coaching tips:
  - watch out for the three resolution "don'ts" (dying, dreaming, and deus ex machina)
  - resolution should follow close on the heels of climax

- Develop plans for an orderly write-a-thon conclusion. Writing athletes will finish at different times and you need to have options for those who are finished. It's important to decide together what you will do so that you can avoid confusion at the end. Possible options are
  - having writers begin a partner evaluation process (Appendix 10)
  - rereading and rewriting draft one
  - recopying manuscripts to make them readable
  - typing manuscripts into the computer
  - story illustration
  - taking those who are done outside so coaches can focus on those who've not yet finished
  - having students who have completed draft one help those who haven't
- Discuss a completion plan. Each writing athlete needs a feeling of completion at the end of their work. You might want to provide this by
  - having a coach, other than the one they've worked with, witness and sign off their story
  - have another child hear the completed work
- Plan new roles for coaches whose groups are completed. They might
  - become a roving coach, helping less-able writers catch up
  - become a check-out coach, doing final manuscript reading
  - monitor outside play
  - monitor partner evaluation
  - prepare the winners' circle party
- Plan your celebratory winners' circle. Try to save at least half an hour to celebrate. Elements that have satisfied writing athletes are:
  - feasting on baked goods

- presenting a certificate of completion with a handshake and announcement of story title and creating author
- placing a handmade "gold medal" around the necks of those who finish (i.e., everyone)
- cheering for ourselves
- having a wrap-up discussion to savor the learning while basking in the glow of triumph
- reading a final book
- announcing a write-a-thon follow-up plan (see Chapter 15)

## Group Coaching on Resolution

This should be a brief session. Write-a-thoners are tired and you want to save all the time you can for writing. Conclude the book you've been reading all day. *Pink and Say* ends with the two boys being torn apart (make sure your visual appreciators notice how Polacco focuses on hands throughout) and then the narrator tells what happened—how Say was released from Andersonville prison months later, weighing no more than seventy-eight pounds, but went on to die an old man while Pinkus Aylee was hung within hours of arriving at Andersonville and his body thrown into a lime pit. Because Pinkus died without family, birth, or death certificates to remember him, Polacco ends the book with a plea to readers to "say his name out loud and vow to remember him always."

Resolution discussion of this book might include such questions as

- What is the feeling you're left with?
- What makes the ending powerful?
- The main character dies. Is Polacco breaking one of three "don'ts"? There is a difference between killing a character off because you can't solve the problem and death as a logical part of the resolution.
- How does the resolution fit with the rest of the book?

Put the story you've read through the resolution checklist before challenging your atheletes to complete the resolution challenge (Appendix 10, page 133) which examines the believability of the ending and makes sure the writer's character has solved the problem.

##  Last Minute Miracles

The writers will have two afternoon sessions with one break. Except for children who've had to leave because of illness, I've always had all writers finish. The afternoon is a flurry of completion and that is why having a completion plan is so important.

Amid the flurry there are special times I savor. One is the working of last-minute miracles. I remember one child finishing up and I asked her, "Are you happy with your story?"

She told me yes, but her accompanying shrug told me she wasn't completely satisfied. I was unfamiliar with her story, but when I read through it, I immediately knew why she wasn't satisfied—and how to fix it. Her story was about a puppy who was kidnapped by a two year old, but because the villain was so young, she couldn't be the mean bully that the story needed. In a matter of moments we'd changed the villain's age and tinkered with her dialogue and actions so that the story was completely pleasing to the writer.

Some of my other moments of joy come from seeing children of lower abilities experience themselves as "real" writers who have written an in-depth story that makes sense. "I wrote a real story!" one young writer told me.

## The Final Celebration

Make sure that you leave enough time at your write-a-thon's end for a proper celebration. I have never felt anything in a classroom that comes close to the exhausted, exhilarated satisfaction at the end of a write-a-thon. Coaches and writers deserve time to savor the victory, admire the hard work, and celebrate both!

The children are always proud when they step up to receive their certificates of completion (see Appendix 12), hear their titles and names spoken aloud, bow their heads to receive their medals, and are applauded by their teammates. They also love the partying, but make sure that you leave time for a wrap-up session.

## Wrapping it Up

The wrap-up is always my favorite part of the winners' circle. When your writers are still glowing with victory but can still remember some of the agonies and joys of creation, you can create an arena for incredibly powerful talks that would be hard to replicate in any other classroom learning situation. As head coach, this is when you harvest the seeds you've been planting throughout the process and when you accept the bounty that your team's hard work has produced. It would be hard to recount all the incredible wrap-ups I've had, but I want to show some of the questions that I use to lead into talks and some of the amazing answers I've received.

- "How did you write your stories?" This question led one class to speak about the differing processes of creation and seeing how each student approached the writing process. In these days of differentiated teaching and an appreciation of different learning styles, I loved hearing children voice their own opinions of how they best learn. Here were some of their observations:
  - I wrote and then thought about what I wrote and then wrote some more.
  - I thought and imagined for a long time and then wrote.
  - I wrote some, read what I'd written and then I began writing again.
  - I "thought on paper," writing as I thought.
  - I was just in my story, not thinking but just writing.
  - I wrote the whole story and then reread it.
  - I just saw my characters and wrote down what I watched them do.

○ I could hear my characters speaking.

○ [As coach], I admired how the different learning styles were accommodated in this one supportive writing process. I could see some of my writers loved the checklist. Others kept coming back to their story plan. Some would overwrite and then synthesize, some writers simmered, others dashed.

• "How did the write-a-thon compare with the standardized writing test you have to take?" When this question was asked, hands flew into the air with groans of remembrance. The tone of the conversation of these fourth graders made me see the difference between writing that produced anxiety and panic and writing that produced pleasure. They valued

○ having the time to really think about their characters

○ being able to develop their own stories and not having to write about the same thing as everyone else

○ not having the pressures of time

○ not feeling like they were being graded

○ having the support of the coaches

• "What helped you during the Write-a-thon, what advice would you give to other writing athletes?" When this was asked in a fifth-grade class, the comments tumbled out:

○ have a clear mind

○ don't rush the story

○ get a lot of sleep

○ read your work over

○ really plan before you write

○ put things in good order so they fit together

○ stick with one character

- "What was hard for you?" One class discussed the following issues:
  - getting everything to fit together right
  - solving the problem my character got in
  - making the conflict get worse in a way that made sense
  - getting to really know a character
  - having the coaches tell you what to do
- "What did you enjoy?" A third-grade class told me they liked
  - the pleasure of being able to work on something without interruption
  - having a long period of time to concentrate on something
  - feeling like a real author
  - feeling that really hard work was worth it, or as one child put it: "I never worked so hard and I've never felt so good about it!"

"Never quit on writing!" one child crowed while his classmates laughed.

I end the write-a-thon wrap-up by accenting the ongoing process of writing. For me it's a life-long passion, and a first draft is more of a beginning than an ending. I have had numerous parents and teachers tell me that the write-a-thon changed their students' lives forever—after the experience these students thought of themselves as writers and critiqued every piece of literature with a voice of experience and wrote with a sense of story.

I am always astounded by wrap-up comments. They could have been made by writers of any age. I realize that I've met my goal of having children understand that they are a part of the writing community—that they are writers. I know the write-a-thon has changed their self-concepts when they come together and offer up the kinds of remarks made by those who know because they have been there!

# Draft Two
# and Beyond

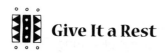 **Give It a Rest**

When runners finish a marathon, they have to have a postrace recovery period before beginning to train again. Most writers give their manuscripts a chance to cool, relishing completion before returning to look at their work through new, more critical eyes. This seems especially important for young writers when you realize they've seldom faced such a demanding learning situation. Rather than risk writing burnout, give them at least a week before beginning draft two. Let them enjoy the victory before they approach the task of revising and editing.

## Moving on to Draft Two

Draft two is a very different process than the creative imagining of draft one. To a write-a-thoner, draft one will have the feel of a complete story. It probably is more complete than most stories they have written, but draft two is essential to true completion.

Creating draft two means looking at the story as a whole: shaping, discovering weaknesses, and increasing the strength of words and ideas. In draft two you evaluate what you've got and then decide what you need to do to get the story to the next stage of completion. If many students have not had a chance to go through partner evaluation (Appendix 11), you might use this to initiate your post–write-a-thon revising.

Completing a write-a-thon deserves a special kind of honoring. One way to show that honor is by having individual meetings with every writer. It's a lot of work but worth every bit of the energy spent. It's amazing to see how writers are willing to learn when their own product is the focus.

I prepare for these individual meetings by typing up manuscripts and triple spacing them to allow room for editing. Many times, older grade levels can type up their own stories, and you'll probably have volunteers to help you with classes that aren't as technologically capable or advantaged.

I go through each manuscript by reading it aloud with the writer and working through large and small problems. I like to tell the story of my friend, author Lee Wardlaw, who writes the most authentic dialogue I've ever encountered in children's books. She records all her chapters into a tape machine and the mechanical distance helps her judge whether her dialogue works or not.

Young writers thrill at seeing their stories in print, hearing them read aloud from a printed page, and having an adult consider seriously the strengths and weaknesses. Generally, during this process I do most of the actual physical rewriting. This breaks the pattern of traditional rewrites in which students moan and groan as they struggle to correct all the teacher's red marks on their manuscripts. This is a discussion from writer to writer. When I take on the writing, it also allows the young writer to attend to thoughts rather than on manual tasks. It also saves time. When I type in editing, I can read my scrawls better than student scribbles.

Changes are both small and large. My editing and revising is meant to challenge them to their next level of capability. Some perform fairly substantial rewrites, while others make minor adjustments. If you see weaknesses occurring in a number of students' writings, it makes sense to give a class minilesson. Use examples to help make your points. Below are some examples of the reoccurring weaknesses I find in working on draft two.

- Words, words, words.
  - Verbs should sparkle with activity. In "Kesha went right away to get an ambulance," *went* could become *dashed* or *sprinted*.
  - Descriptions may be unclear or flat; "'You can come in now,'" said the scary old nurse." Scary how? This is a great opening for a description of her, and it would help set the mood for the evil dentist's office she works in.
  - Confusion may lead to switching between past or present tenses. One write-a-thon phenomenon I've noticed is that even coaches who are scribing may incorrectly switch from past to present tense. The demand of writing as fast as you are thinking often produces a switch to present tense.
  - Dialogue may need contractions. This is a problem easily solved by reading aloud. People don't say, "I will be right up," but "I'll be right up."
- Characters.
  - Characters get dropped. In one story, Marie saved a bully from choking by getting gum out of her mouth, but the story ends "everyone was Marie's friend" and there's no mention of Marie's tormentor.
  - Characters drop in. A character never before introduced, suddenly springs into the story. I remember one write-a-thoner who brought in five new characters in four paragraphs!
  - Viewpoints change. We move from a first person to third person in the blink of an eye. We have a flying pig's owner telling the story and then suddenly we're in the body of the pig.
  - Characters lack discerning details. Writers often use short hand. For instance, rather than telling us that Slimy the tap-dancing salamander "learned to deal with Francis the Fat Frog," show how Francis, a frog, tortured him on several occasions and how Slimy dealt with it.
  - No character reaction. A frog has all his baby frogs eaten and, without expressing any emotion, goes off to dig another hole to live in.

- What's the motivation? A character needs a reason for doing things in a story. One child had a boy haunted by having to find his dead mother's necklace, but never having explained its significance made the whole story unbelieveable

- Where am I?
  - The setting is not clear at all. In the first paragraph of one inventive story, for example, a character is captured from Mars, taken to Earth, North Carolina, and then college! Such changes make my head whirl as if I'm in orbit!

- Timing is everything.
  - Conflict appears before motivation. A turtle expresses fears of being trapped in a NASA spaceship before we learn that he wants to get back to his planet more than anything and that's why he's gotten aboard.
  - Too much happens without explanation. This problem is the opposite of having too many details. One writer ended a paragraph with the death of the character's parents and his relocation to a foster home. In the next paragraph we hear that "A few years later, Froggie married Fern." What happened to his childhood? I bet he had some intense feelings the writer never utilized. Sometimes, young writers who run out of time try to tell the many years of their character's life in the last line of the story.
  - Change occurs in a story too quickly. I don't believe that a character would go from telling her mother "Mom I hate you, just hate you!" to "Mom, let's compromise" without a dramatic event making the change. Without transitions, I can't believe the transformation.

Sometimes I find opportunity to pass on wisdom I've learned from other writers;

- Sid Fleishman, a well-known children's book author, once advised "point your finger to the hole!" This occurs when you've got a story flaw that you explain within the context of your story before your reader can wonder. If a character pops back in the story, you might explain the absence by saying that character had just returned from vacation.

- Upping the emotional ante—strengthening a story by making the conflict more intense. You could show a cruel queen has changed by having her step in front of a servant who's going to be slapped rather than having her defend the servant in an argument. A time deadline, can also help—something that has to be invented within twenty-four hours will increase drama.

## ⣿ Moving Beyond Draft Two

Where do we go from here? There are a number of different directions you can move in. For writers who become hooked on perfecting their work, I've composed a resource for those approaching a third draft (see Appendix 13).

Stories can be used as departure points, creating opportunities to allow for different learning styles and student strengths.

- Those given to drawing can create an illustrated book. They can learn everything from how effective page breaks keep readers wanting more to removing some text when pictures would be more effective.

- A manuscript could also be transformed into a play, which is especially easy if the writer shines at dialogue. Then young writers can go off in different directions, creating costumes and stage sets and selecting actors.

Once I've completed draft two with writers and added the changes to their manuscripts, they might like to find affirmation from their classmates by reading their story aloud. I like to compile the stories into a class collection. Students seem proud of their own work and of the collection too.

 **Publish Me, Please!**

Many times young writers ask me if they can get their story published. I see that as a perfect opening to teaching them about the submission process and moving into a different kind of writing with persuasive cover letters. Young writers savor the feeling of professionalism as they learn about SASE's (prononced "sassies," the self-addressed stamped envelopes you include as a courtesy to publishers) and researching possible places to submit. Happily, children seem so pleased to receive any mail that they don't seem to mind the rejections as much as adults. And, as I tell writers of all ages, a manuscript can't be published if you don't send it off!

The best resource I've found for children who want to publish is Kathy Henderson's *Market Guide for Young Writers,* (published by Writer's Digest Books, it is periodically updated). Henderson does a wonderful job of describing every phase of the publishing process. Information about her book and possible places for submission are listed in Appendix 14. Consider also local children's papers or even contacting your newspaper about publication of some or all of the stories.

There are other ways to publish and I stress this with children because there are strong odds against commercial publishing success. I tell them that I've written twenty-seven children's books, and submitted my work for over fifteen years but only managed to have one children's book published. But I do read my unpublished work with classes.

Publishing, in the truest sense of the word, really means sharing with others. Sharing can be done by putting the class anthology in the library, their classroom, or in other classes where the students have wondered what this write-a-thon business has been all about.

# Cool Down!
## Relief, Rest, and Reflection

Runners end a marathon with relief, rest, and reflection. Crossing the finish line of this book, I am filled with the same feelings. I have the relief that comes at the end of a race well run. It was a challenge to capture in words a process borne so miraculously, for the metaphor had such power that the original write-a-thon forms tumbled out of my computer keys in a single weekend. I also felt charged with recording the evolution, for every write-a-thoner—coach or child—added new growth or excitement to the original run. The race itself was demanding, but there was exhilaration in every footfall. I can proudly say that I did not hit the wall once!

I can rest now. I can relax as torch bearer, knowing that I've passed on the fiery ideas to subsequent runners. I rest knowing that they will run this race differently, discover new traditions and glories while experiencing some of the same triumphs that I've shared with children and adults.

Athletes are given to self-improvement. I have picked apart my own strategies to make them more successful and have been genuine about my failures. I must remember too that after being in and out of classrooms for twenty years I have never experienced the kind of energy that a write-a-thon generates. It fights for so much of what our modern culture steals from our children. The write-a-thon

- Gives them back their right to explore inner landscapes
- Shows them that investment in a long-term project is rewarding beyond what they might have imagined and that hard work is worth the investment
- Creates opportunities for students to prove to themselves that they can step up to a challenge and meet it
- Teaches that time and learning do not always have to be separated into small fragments
- Gives them the constant support of others who are committed to their success
- Allows them to discover strengths they never knew they had.

My last reflections are for you, the ones who will carry the torch. Remember the words of the coach who told us to "Remember the watermelon. You don't eat it all at once, but one bite at a time!" Above all, have fun!

# *Bibliography*
## *Children's Books to Inspire Writing*

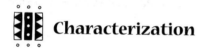 **Characterization**

Altman, Linda, *Amelia's Road* (Lee and Low, 1994; grades 3–5)

Buehner, Caralyn, *Fanny's Dream* (Dial, 1996; grades 4–6)

Coleman, Evelyn, *The Foot Warmer and the Crow* (Macmillan, 1994; grades 4–6)

Coleman, Evelyn, *The Glass Bottle Tree* (Orchard, 1995; grades 4–6)

Erdrich, Louise, *Grandmother's Pigeon* (Hyperion, 1996; grades 3–5)

Harshman, Marc, *Uncle James* (Dutton, 1993; grades 4–6)

Hoffman, Mary, *Boundless Grace* (Dial, 1994; grades 2–3)

Jackson, Ellen, *Cinder Edna* (Lothrop, 1994; grades 3–6)

Johnson, Dolores, *Your Dad Was Just Like You* (Macmillan, 1993; grades 2–4)

Kurtz, Jane, *Miro in the Kingdom of the Sun* (Houghton Mifflin, 1996; grades 2–6)

Mochizuki, Ken, *Baseball Saved Us; Heroes* (Lee and Low, 1993 ; grades 4–6)

Polacco, Patricia, *Pink and Say* (Philomel, 1994; grades 4–adult)

Polacco, Patricia, *Babushka Baba Yaga* (Philomel, 1993; grades 3–5)

San Souci, Daniel, *Sukey and the Mermaid* (Four Winds Press, 1992; grades 4–6)

Steig, William, *Brave Irene*, (Farrar, 1986; grades 2–4)

Steptoe, John, *Mufaro's Beautiful Daughters* (Lothrop, 1987; grades 2–4)

Tynia, Thomassie, *Feliciana Feydra Le Roux* (Little Brown, 1994; grades 2–3)

##  Senses and Setting

Anderson, Janet, *The Key into Winter* (Whitman, 1994; grades 3–6)

Casley, Judith, *Harry and Willy and Carrothead* (Greenwillow, 1991; grades 2–3)

Coerr, Eleanor, *Sadako* (Putnam, 1993; grades 4–6)

Coleman, Evelyn, *White Socks Only* (Whitman, 1996; grades 4–6)

Collington, Peter, *The Coming of Surfman* (Knopf, 1993; grades 4–6)

Hastings, Selina, *Sir Gwain and the Loathly Lady* (Morrow, 1987; grades 4–6)

Heide & Gilliland, *The Day of Ahmed's Secret* (Lothrop, 1990; grades 3–5)

Isaacs, Ann, *Swamp Angel* (Dutton, 1994; grades 3–6)

Kurtz, Jane, *Fire on the Mountain* (Simon & Schuster, 1994; grades 4–6)

Mills, Lauren, *Rag Coat* (Little Brown, 1991; grades 3–6)

Mills, Lauren and Nolan, Dennis, *Fairy Wings* (Little Brown, 1995; grades 3–5)

Rappaport, Doreen, *The New King* (Dial, 1996; grades 4–6)

Turner, Ann, *Nettie's Trip South* (Macmillan, 1987; grades 3–6)

Turner, Ann, *Katie's Trunk* (Macmillan, 1992; grades 3–5)

Watson, Mary, *The Butterfly Seeds* (Tambourine, 1995; grades 3–5)

## Conflict

Bull, Emma, *The Princess and the Lord of Night* (HBJ, 1994; grades 3–5)

Bunting, Eve, *The Man Who Could Call Down Owls* (Clarion, 1984; grades 3–5)

Bunting, Eve, *The Terrible Things: An Allegory of the Holocaust* (Jewish Publications, 1989; grades 4–6)

Echewa, Obinkaram, T., *The Ancestor Tree* (Lodestar, 1994; grades 4–6)

Hooks, William, *Freedom's Fruit* (Knopf, 1995; grades 4–6)

Innocenti, Roberto, *Rose Blanche* (Creative Education, 1985; grades 4–6)

Jackson, Isaac, *Somebody's New Pajamas* (Dial, 1996; grades 3–6)

Johnson, Dolores, *Now Let Me Fly* (Macmillan, 1993; grades 4–6)

Lester, Julius, *The Man Who Knew Too Much* (Clarion, 1994; grades 4–6)

Scieszka, Jon, *The True Story of the Three Little Pigs* (Viking, 1989; grades 1–6)

Scieszka, Jon, *The Frog Prince Continued* (Viking, 1991, grades 1–6)

Shannon, David, *How Georgie Radbourn Saved Baseball* (Scholastic, 1994; grades 3–6)

Wood, Audrey, *Heckedy Peg* (HBJ, 1987; grades 1–3)

Yep, Laurence, *The Man Who Tricked a Ghost* (Bridgewater Books, 1993; grades 3–6)

# Dialogue

Alexander, Lloyd, *The Fortune-Teller* (Dutton, 1992; grades 3–5)

Fox, Mem, *Wilfred Gordon McDonald Partridge* (Kane Miller, 1985; grades 2–4)

Johnston, Tony, *The Cowboy and the Black-Eyed Pea* (Putnam, 1993; grades 2–4)

Lester, Julius, *Sam and the Tigers* (Dial, 1996; grades 1–5)

Martin & Archambault, *Knots on a Counting Rope* (Holt, 1987; grades 3–5)

Palatini, Margie, *Piggie Pie* (Clarion, 1995; grades 3–6)

Polacco, Patricia, *Chicken Sunday* (Philomel, 1992; grades 3–6)

Yorinks, Arthur, *Company's Coming* (Crown, 1988; grades 2–4)

(Please note that often a book may fit into more than one category; also some of these might be longer picture books that you would choose to use in training instead of in the Write-a-thon itself.)

# Runners' Bibliography

 **Children's Books**

 **Runners**

Aaseng, Nathan, *Florence Griffith Joyner* (Lerner, 1989; grades 3–6). Joyner's biography tells of difficult beginnings and a creative individuality that battle all odds. Detailed accounts of races add sports drama to the personal style of this runner.

Fogel, Julianna, *Wesley Paul, Marathon Runner* (Lippincott, 1979; grades 3–6). The true story of Wesley Paul, a nine-year-old marathon runner. Told in the words of a child who ran the New York Marathon in less than three hours. This picture book has short text on every page.

Henkel, Cathy, *Mary Decker* (Children's Press, 1984; grades 3–6). An easy-to-read biography of Decker, who won an Olympic medal. The biography ends before her tragic fall during an Olympic event. The focus is on how she keeps on despite bad luck and accidents. Many black-and-white photos with large print.

Jennings, Jay, *Long Shots: Sports Triumphs* (Silver Burdette, 1990; grades 3–7). Wilma Rudolph is one of five athletes in this book who "beat the odds." Ten pages of this collection are devoted to telling how she overcame poverty, disease that withered her leg and kept her in braces for years, and an early pregnancy to win three gold medals at the 1960 Olympics.

Krull, Kathleen, *Wilma Unlimited* (Harcourt, Brace, Jovanovich, 1996; grades 2–5). Texture marks the artistry of this picture book biography. Krull, a seasoned nonfiction writer, makes this woman's life of determination spring from the pages as she tells how the famous runner fought discrimination of race and gender. Caldecott Award-winning artist David Diaz represents the elements of Rudolph's life with amazing collages.

Rennert, Rick, *Jesse Owens* (Chelsea House, 1992; grades 3–6). Full of black-and-white photos, this biography gives a significant portion of the book over to Owens's famous win of three gold medals at the 1936 Olympics. The book also traces Owens from poor rural beginnings through devoted coaches who taught him about the sport to his sportsmanship, which was even greater than his athletic prowess. It even discusses his difficulty in returning to normal life after his great fame.

 **Crossing the Curriculum**

Parker, Steve, *Running a Race: How You Walk, Run, and Jump* (Watts, 1991; grades 3–6). Are you looking for ways to help your write-a-thon cross the curriculum? This book examines how your body operates while racing, looking at the skeletal, muscular, and circulatory systems. It's also a great resource for metaphors.

**Adult Resource Books**

Bloom, Marc, *The Marathon: What It Takes to Go the Distance* (Holt, 1981). Filled with stories from the past and present, it includes the stories of Bucky Cox, a five-year-old marathon runner, and Rainear, the runner who completed a marathon after being shot. Metaphors abound in the chapter of psychology and in stories of well-known marathoners like Frank Shorter and Grete Waitz. There is much technical information you won't need, but it is a great book to skim.

Campbell, Gail, *Marathon: The World of the Long-Distance Athlete,* (Sterling, 1977). The first fifty pages of this book are devoted to long-distance runners and races. This includes profiles of runners from around the world (like Mexico's Tarahuma Indians, who pursue a deer until it drops dead of exhaustion) and looks at specific personalities (like Bill Emmerton, who crossed Death Valley while the temperature was 135 degrees); or Ethiopian Abebe Bikila, who ran the 1960 Olympic marathon barefoot), and describes famous races like the 1928 transcontinental 3,422-mile "Bunion Derby."

Fixx, James, *The Complete Book of Running* (Random, 1977). Though Fixx writes of many aspects of running, there are plenty of marathon images in this very readable book. There's more information than you'll need, but you can clearly skip the more technical parts. The book is filled with fascinating material.

Higdon, Hal, *Marathon: The Ultimate Training and Racing Guide* (Rodale Press, 1993). This book describes much of the marathoning experience, revealing metaphors easily applied to a write-a-thon (like "hitting the wall" and "runner's glow"). There is a good description of history and differing styles of running. This has strategies from over fifty coaches and runners and is quite specific. For write-a-thon purposes, it's a book to be skimmed, not read cover to cover.

Temple, Cliff, *The Marathon Made Easier: A Safe and Simple Guide to Distance Running* (Atheneum, 1982). Of greatest use are the first two chapters, which are filled with anecdotal stories of the kinds of people who run races (e.g. the World's Fastest Waiter who dresses in full waiter garb and even carries a tray with water balanced on it; and Wally Scott, a blind runner) and other stories that give a strong emotional tone.

Waitz, Grete, and Averbuch, Gloria, *Grete Waitz: World Class* (Warner Books, 1986). This personal view of one marathoner's life presents views of health Norweigan-style and many emotional metaphors, including the constant pressures, consistency, goal setting, nervousness, and focus.

# *Volunteer Form 1*

A class write-a-thon is coming to _____

(name of your school/class)

_____

(dates)

We Need Coaches! We Need You!

We are organizing a class write-a-thon and we need coaches. Our write-a-thon is like a running marathon because our "writing athletes" will endure two days of nearly uninterrupted time to write. They will come away from the experience with the triumph of having completed an entire story. To help our young players, we are asking that coaches come and assist them while they write to their goals.

Of course our writing athletes will benefit, but the coaches will too. It's a miraculous creative process that's hard to describe. As former coaches have said,

I'm not usually the kind of parent who likes to volunteer in the classroom, but the write-a-thon was the most rewarding, most fun volunteer experience I've ever had. It was unlike anything I'd ever participated in.

I loved seeing the excitement of the children, their dedication to the hard work, then their resulting pride and joy in what they created. Even as an adult, I was fascinated by the way the creative process developed and made sense in the context of uninterrupted time.

For me, and for most of the students, the experience was meaningful, demanding, and at the end gave a true feeling of the kind of special success that only comes after you've invested your mind, heart, and soul in a project.

The requirements are
- to attend a coaching-the-coaches one-hour meeting on _____ (date), where you will be prepped for the experience, be given a list of expectations, and begin the fun! (Refreshments and fun provided.)
- to coach for at least one day.

We also need other kinds of support, so please read through the list and see if there's anything you can do.

Name _____

home phone _____ work phone _____

_____ I am interested in coaching the write-a-thon

_____ I can't be a write-a-thon coach, but I'd be happy to support our writing athletes

and coaches by providing snacks for children and/or adults. I'll prepare the snack

for _____ children and _____ adults.

_____ I'd be happy to make a healthy snack (e.g., orange slices, fruit kabobs,

celery and peanut butter, carrots with ranch dressing).

_____ I'd be happy to bring juice.

_____ I'd really like to bake something for the final celebration (cake, cookies,

brownies).

_____ I'd be happy to type up some of the children's work.

_____ I can make/buy medals for the winning writers (this will be all students in the class).

_____ I can come and supervise children during a break period so the coaches can rest.

_____ I can make certificates of completion for all the writing athletes (the head coach

will contact you with directions).

_____ I have run a marathon, triathlon, or participated in a long-distance race and

would be happy to come and share my experience to excite the young writing

athletes before the write-a-thon.

_____ I'd be happy to prepare an extra lunch for a coach.

_____ I can't give time, but I'd be happy to contribute $1 to $3 to help cover the

cost of copying and supplies (please return your money with this form).

_____ I have another idea about how I can participate in the write-a-thon. I'd like to:

_____

I can coach for:

_____ two whole days _____ one whole day _____ 1/2 day

My best days are:

_____ Monday _____ Tuesday _____ Wednesday _____ Thursday _____ Friday

If you're interested in coaching, please complete the following form so we can get a sense of how to make you most comfortable and successful.

I like to read

Strongly Agree     Agree     Doesn't Apply     Disagree     Strongly Disagree

I like to write

Strongly Agree     Agree     Doesn't Apply     Disagree     Strongly Disagree

I am good at problem solving with children

Strongly Agree      Agree      Doesn't Apply      Disagree      Strongly Disagree

I'm not afraid to help a child who's gotten off track find his/her way back onto the course

Strongly Agree      Agree      Doesn't Apply      Disagree      Strongly Disagree

I most like to read

\_\_\_\_\_ nonfiction

\_\_\_\_\_ fiction

\_\_\_\_\_ mysteries

\_\_\_\_\_ science fiction

\_\_\_\_\_ biographies

I am most comfortable working with children who are

\_\_\_\_\_ above-average writers

\_\_\_\_\_ average writers

\_\_\_\_\_ below-average writers

\_\_\_\_\_ a mix of different writing abilities

\_\_\_\_\_ it doesn't matter

I'd most like to be involved in coaching

\_\_\_\_\_ the planning and pre-writing

\_\_\_\_\_ the first draft

\_\_\_\_\_ all of it

**APPENDIX**

# 4

# *Coaches' Playsheet 1*

Title of focus book:

_____

Author of focus book:

_____

Choose a focus character:

_____

Use illustration and text to select the two most important physical attributes of your focus character.

_____

_____

How would you know this character if she or he walked into the room?

_____

What does this character want more than anything?

_____

What gets in the character's way?

_____

What's going to happen to the character after the pages of the book close?

_____

APPENDIX

# 5

# *Coaches' Playsheet 2*

1. Choose a character from those we created together.

   _____

2. Tell two important things you know about that character's appearance and two important things about that character's behavior.

   _____

   _____

   _____

   _____

3. What does the character want more than anything in the world?

_____

_____

4. What problem is in the way of your character getting what she or he wants?

_____

_____

5. Tell three ways the problem gets worse.

_____

_____

_____

6. Now that you've gotten your character in trouble, how are you going to get her or him out of trouble?

_____

_____

_____

_____

APPENDIX

**6**

# Coaches' Overview, Schedule, and Tips

## Day 1 Goal: A Story Plan

Mile 1: Character Development

Mile 2: Conflict

Mile 3: How Does the Problem Get Worse

Mile 4: Resolution

## Day 2 Goal: A First Draft

Mile 5: Writing a Grabber First Line

Mile 6: Writing a Grabber First Paragraph

Mile 7: The Middle Miles: Don't Let Your Middle Sag

Mile 8: The Home Stretch: Conflict Worsens to Climax

Mile 9: The Finish Line: Resolution

The Winners' Circle

 **Overall Coaching Tips**

- Coaches are looking for consistency. Characters should act in ways that make sense.

- Coaches are not afraid to step in and offer suggestions. Some students may have troubles, don't be afraid to really coach them through to a story that works. You can inspire your athletes to greater heights with your thoughtfulness and help them think.

- If you're feeling in over your head call for the head coach.

- When an athlete hits the wall, don't be afraid to help them out. If they need you to take over the physical job of writing, go ahead. Their consistent thinking process is what's most important. Keep letting them know they can do it!

- If you're feeling that you can't get through to an athlete, another coach's style may work better . . . so call in the head coach if you're feeling stuck.

- Don't let the writer solve the problem too easily.

- Make sure your writers are staying with their story.

- If your Write-a-thoner is wandering off in all kinds of complexities help him/her back to a simpler plot.

- If you get a sense that a child can work more deeply, urge them to do so. Press capable students for active verbs, images, descriptions.

- Tell students if you find something unbelievable or incomplete. Have them state their reasons and allow only what they can defend.

# Coaches' Guide

 **Goal for Day I: Develop a Writing Plan**

1. Coaching Session: What is a write-a-thon? Explain the write-a-thon set up: water stations, aid stations, coaching sessions and goals. Conclude with a discussion of character, using a book to reference the concept. Play the character game.

2. Student writing Mile 1: Character: The basics.

3. Aid station check-in: Coaches meet with writers. At this point, you want to ensure that their characters make sense, that they're starting to have a sense of the character, and that they aren't creating a cast of thousands.

4. Water station and coaching session: snack, read a book, and have a mini-lesson on motivation.

5. Student writing Mile 1: Character. What is your character like in the world?

6. Aid station check-in: Coaches meet with the writers. Does this newest information make sense in terms of the character they have set up?

7. Student writing Mile 1: Characters. Your character on the inside.

8. Aid station check-in: Coaches meet with the writers. Does this newest information make sense in terms of the character they have set up?

9. Water Station: Recess!

10. Student writing: Mile 1 (continued). Characters on the inside.

11. Aid station check-in: Coaches meet with the writers. Does this newest information make sense in terms of the character they have set up?

12. Coaching Session: Read a book and have a mini-lesson on conflict.

13. Mile 2: Conflict.

14. Aid station check-in: Coaches meet with the writers. Does the conflict come out of the character they have created or is it pasted on? Is this a new or old problem? Help students fit the conflict with the character if it doesn't.

15. Mile 3: Plot. How does the problem get worse?

16. Water station: Lunch.

17. Aid station check-in: Coaches meet with the writers. This time it's really important to check the logic of the way the problem unfolds. Does one problem follow another rather than just being thrown in? Do they follow a natural progression, building from bad to worse?

18. Coaching Session: Read a book and have a minilesson on resolution.

19. Mile 4: Resolution. How does the problem get better?

20. Aid station check-in. Does the resolution fit with the problem and with the character? Is it logical? Does it avoid the three "Don'ts" of dying, dreaming, and *deus ex machina?*

21. Coaching session: Pep rally, check-in, and round-up. Give the homework assignment: come up with a great grabber sentence.

# Goal for Day 2: A Complete First Draft

1. Coaching session: Grabber first lines. Share homework.

2. Student writing: Mile 5: Miracle Mile. Write down your grabber first line.

3. Coaching session: grabber first paragraphs.

4. Student writing: Mile 6: Writing a grabber first paragraph.

5. Aid station: First of all make sure the writers are skipping lines. Does the first paragraph make sense? Does it have a strong beginning? Can you tell that it's leading somewhere? Here are some comments that may help the students evaluate their grabber paragraphs:

   a. Will it hold your readers' attention?

   b. Does it tell who, what, where, when and why?

   c. Remember, you can go back later and put in more description. For now, you're just getting the ideas down!

   d. Does it all make sense?

      1. Are all the whats, whos, wheres, whens, whys, etc. grouped together?

      2. Does each idea make sense with the idea that went before it?

   Complete and sign First Paragraphs Evaluation.

6. Water station: Recess.

7. Water station: Snack.

8. Coaching session: Developing plot through scenes.

9. Student writing: Mile 7: The Middle Miles. Write your plot in scenes.

10. Aid station. Students should be checking in every two paragraphs. This is probably the most individual part of the process. Some kids will write two paragraphs, some will write two pages. What you want to track here is whether their story is

making sense and following a logical sequence of events. You might also watch tangents. This is the place where they may go off on side journeys that make little sense to the story. Complete and sign Middle Miles Evaluation.

11. Water station: Recess.

12. Coaching session: Tension builds to a climax.

13. Student writing: Mile 8: The home stretch: Tension builds to a climax.

14. Water station: Lunch.

15. Aid station: Students should be checking in every two paragraphs. Complete and sign Home Stretch Evaluation.

16. Coaching session: Resolution.

17. Student writing: Mile 9: The finish line: resolution.

18. Aid station: The finish line and evaluation. Coaches should think about writers satisfying the following checklist:

\_\_\_\_\_ I believe the resolution

\_\_\_\_\_ The resolution makes sense with the rest of the story

\_\_\_\_\_ The way the character solves the problem makes sense

\_\_\_\_\_ The character doesn't die to solve the problem

\_\_\_\_\_ The character doesn't wake up from a dream to solve the problem

\_\_\_\_\_ The character isn't rescued to solve the problem

\_\_\_\_\_ The ending is satisfying (Remember, it doesn't have to be happy)

My favorite part of the ending is _____ .

Complete and sign the Finish Line Evaluation.

# *Volunteer Acknowledgment Form*

Dear _____
(name of volunteer)

As the excitement mounts for our write-a-thon, we are so happy that you've agreed to be a member of our support team! We want to take a moment to be sure that we're properly organized. Please check and make sure we haven't made any mistakes. Our write-a-thon roster shows that you will:

_____ coach _____ write-a-thon athletes
(number of students)

on _____
(day of the week and date)

from _____
(times)

The athletes you'll be coaching are:

_____

_____

_____

_____ provide a snack on _____

(day of the week and date)

please be sure you send a healthy, light snack unless you intend to send something for our final celebration

_____ provide lunch for a coach on _____

(day of the week and date)

_____ supervise breaks

on _____

(day of the week and date)

from _____

(times)

_____ make medals (please deliver them to me by _____ so we'll have them for our final write-a-thon honor ceremony)

_____ make or print certificates of completion (please get them to me on _____ so we'll have them for our write-a-thon honor ceremony)

We also thank those of you who have agreed to type up manuscripts for our athletes. Would you help us by giving us the following information? We'll contact you after the write-a-thon with more specific information

_____ phone (day) _____

_____ phone (evening) _____

_____ I create on Macintosh _____

IBM _____

Thank you for helping to make our write-a-thon a success!

# APPENDIX 9A

# A Basic Schedule for a Two-Day Write-a-thon

This schedule, prepared for an 8:00–2:15 day, could be changed to adapt to other schedules, but will serve as a model on which to base your plan.

## Goal for Day 1: Develop a Writing Plan

| | |
|---|---|
| 8:00–8:10 | Group coaching session and introduction |
| 8:10–8:30 | Group coaching session on character |
| 8:30–9:10 | Mile 1: Student writing on character |
| 9:10–9:25 | Write-a-thoners' recess, preparation of snack, and coaches' check-in |
| 9:25–9:40 | Snack for students, a coach and student check-in, and a group coaching session on motivation |
| 9:40–10:30 | Mile 1: Student writing on character continues |
| 10:30–11:00 | Write-a-thoners' recess and/or PE; coaches meet |
| 11:00–11:20 | Group coaching session on conflict and check-in with coaches and writers |
| 11:20–12:00 | Mile 2: Student writing on conflict |

| 12:00–12:35 | Lunch and movement and coaches' check-in session |
| 12:35–12:40 | Group coaching session on plot: Comments from coaches and writers and focusing pep talk from head coach |
| 12:40–1:15 | Mile 3: Student writing on plot |
| 1:15–1:25 | Student movement, coaches' check-in, and snack preparation |
| 1:25–1:35 | Group coaching session on resolution: Check-in with coaches and writers |
| 1:35–2:05 | Mile 4: Student writing on Resolution |
| 2:05–2:10 | Last coaching session, and homework: Come up with a grabber title and first sentence |

## Goal for Day 2: A Complete First Draft

| 8:05–8:30 | Group coaching session: Check-in with coaches and writers |
| 8:30–9:10 | Mile 5: Student writing on the grabber first line and Mile 6: The grabber first paragraph |
| 9:10–9:25 | Write-a-thoners' recess, preparation of snack, coaches' check-in |
| 9:25–9:40 | A coach and student check-in and group coaching session on story scenes or middle miles |
| 9:40–10:30 | Mile 7: Student writing on the middle miles |
| 10:30–11:00 | Write-a-thoners' recess and/or physical education; coaches' check-in |
| 11:00–11:20 | Coaches' comments: Short group coaching on home stretch |
| 11:20–12:00 | Mile 8: Student writing on the home stretch continues |
| 12:00–12:30 | Lunch and movement and coaching session |
| 12:30–12:45 | Group coaching session: resolution |
| 12:45–1:15 | Mile 9: Student writing on Resolution, peer evaluation, and a check-out with another coach |
| 1:15–1:25 | Student movement, coaches' coaching, and snack preparation |
| 1:25–1:45 | Student writing continues and concludes, peer evaluation and coaches' check-out |
| 1:45–2:10 | Winners' circle ceremony and party! |

# *An Annotated Schedule for a Two-Day Write-a-thon*

## Goal for Day 1: Develop a Writing Plan

8:00–8:10      Group coaching session and introduction

- Introduce coaches and groups; introduce rule 1 of write-a-thon: "Listen to your coach!"
- A write-a-thon is not a marathon: don't race!
- Watch complexity in your story: Keep it simple
- Remember rules of writing: No violence, stealing, or repulsiveness
- Explain how the elements of the day will work:
  - How to get attention
  - What to do when you're waiting for attention
  - Breaks of the day
  - Aid station: Talking to your coach is a necessity

8:10–8:30     Group coaching session on character

- Read a book, play the character game
- Compare a few character questions to the character you've read about
- Ask a few children to speak about how they would answer character questions based on the characters they've developed

8:30–9:10     Mile 1: Student writing on character
9:10–9:25     Write-a-thoners' recess, preparation of snack, and coaches' check-in

- Important to see how they're doing with process at this first check-in; they may have a need to discuss or question specifics of process now that it is in action
- Let coaches know that the write-a-thon is continually evolving and their feedback is important; that they may see their own individual style growing and they should follow it
- Discussion of trends being seen in the children's work
- Specific difficulties with specific children
- Are write-a-thoners checking in?
- Are writing athletes understanding their characters or merely answering questions?
- Coaching problems that need attention?
- Where is the group in their writing?
- Any need for head coaching or writers in trouble?
- Collect comments to mention to whole group
- Speak to coaches of range of writing capability

9:25–9:40     Snack for students, a coach and student check-in, and a group coaching session on motivation
              Time for an open-ended discussion about how the writing is going

- Head coach may speak about trends gleaned from coaches
- Comments from all coaches
- Head coach asks students for questions and comments

Follow with a group coaching session on motivation, which will come at the end of their character planning:

- read a book, focus on motivation
- discuss motivation in previous stories read
- ask write-a-thoners for examples of their characters' motivations

9:40–10:30    Mile 1: Student Writing on character continues
10:30–11:00    Write-a-thoners' recess and/or PE; coaches meet

General coaching questions will always include

- Trends being seen in the work
- Specific difficulties with specific children
- Are the characters beginning to develop?
- Is a consistent character emerging?
- Coaching problems that need attention
- Where is the group in their writing? (you would hope by this point they'd be nearing the end of character development)
- Anyone need the head coach?
- Any children struggling who could use one-to-one coaching?
- Collect comments to mention to whole group

In addition, during this session you might ask

- Did motivation pull characters together?
- Does their newest character information make sense in terms of what they've set up?

- Head coach announces that the next group coaching will cover character's conflict; try to hold most students to conflict before lunch break.
- When checking conflict, make sure it comes out of the character they've created rather than pasting it on. Help students fit the conflict with the character.

11:00–11:20    Group coaching session, check-in with coaches and writers
- Comments from all coaches
- Questions and comments from write-a-thoners
- How many are almost finished with Mile 1?

11:20–12:00    Mile 2: Student writing on conflict
12:00–12:35    Lunch and movement and coaches meet

Ask general coaching questions and be sure to discuss
- As we're moving into plot and the conflict worsens, it's crucial to check the logic of the way the problem unfolds; does one problem follow another rather than just being thrown in and do they follow a natural progression of getting worse and worse?

12:35–12:40    Group coaching session: comments from coaches and writers and focusing pep talk from head coach
12:40–1:15    Mile 3: Student writing on plot
1:15–1:25    Student movement, coaches' coaching, and snack preparation

Coaching questions include
- Are their story lines making sense?
- Are there coaching problems that need attention?
- Where is the group in their writing?
- Any need for head coaching?

- Who's in danger of not finishing?
- Collect comments to mention to the whole group
- Head coach prepares for resolution. Make sure resolution fits with the problem and with the character; does it avoid the three "don'ts" of dying, dreaming, and *deus ex machina?*

| | |
|---|---|
| 1:25–1:35 | Group coaching session: Check-ins and resolution |
| 1:35–2:05 | Mile 4: Student writing on resolution |
| 2:05–2:10 | Last coaching session and homework: Come up with a grabber title and first sentence |

## Goal for Day 2: A Complete First Draft

8:05–8:30    Group coaching session: Check-in with coaches and writers

- Check on yesterday's conclusion; who needs help finishing?
- Comments from coaches about the day ahead
- Introduction
  - Skip lines
  - Different pacing of athletes; be sure to check in with coaches at aid stations or when needed
- Check in on homework
- Students share grabber titles and first lines
- Coaches should gather titles for certificates

Group coaching session on setting (grabber first paragraph)

- Describe elements of setting, not just place and time; discuss the importance of including elements that will affect your character (e.g., big or small town; happy or unhappy family)
- Use only your strongest points, though you might know much more
- Brief discussion of descriptive writing (using senses, similes, metaphors, active verbs)
- Include in introductory paragraphs
  - Who? (your character)
  - Where? (where the story takes place)
  - When? (time of year, time of life)
  - What? (give a hint of the problem at hand)
  - Why? (Why characters feel the way they do about life or conflicts)
- Read a book that shows a grabber first paragraph
- Importance of "show, don't tell" includes writing challenges such as
  - Can you get the time across without just telling the date?
  - Instead of saying your character is a glutton, have her or him wander to the refrigerator and pig out several times in the first paragraph
  - Including your character's feelings or reactions to the setting will strengthen the story; character anger, disappointment, and fear are important parts of setting. Your characters' strengths are also important to the setting.
  - There should be at least a hint of the problem.

| | |
|---|---|
| 8:30–9:10 | Mile 5: Student writing on the grabber first line and Mile 6: The grabber first paragraph |
| 9:10–9:25 | Write-a-thoners' recess, preparation of snack, coaches meet |

Coaches' check-in includes:

- Who's not finished with story plan from day one?
- Gather comments on trends being seen
- Check-in as to how writers are transitioning and note those having problems
- Discuss the importance of elements in the story's beginning
- Success will be measured by First Paragraph Evaluation, these need to be checked and signed off before children continue
- Warning about coming sessions, which is where different student styles and capabilities will show up.

9:25–9:40    A snack for students, a coaches' and student check-in, and a group coaching session on each story's middle

- Comments and questions of coaches and children
- Read a book; stress how all scenes in the story move it along to the ending; those that don't might be excluded
- With limited time, it's important not to become lost in one scene; look back on the story plan for pacing
- Students should check in with coaches every one to three paragraphs
- Watch for undeveloped scenes
- Watch your write-a-thon guide for clues

9:40–10:25    Mile 7: Student writing on the middle miles
10:30–11:00    Write-a-thoners' recess or physical education—coaches meet

- Assessment of where groups are
- Need for head coach?
- Importance of sticking to previous day's plan
- Importance of moving athletes along

11:00–11:10   Short group coaching on home stretch

- Warn of the potential for hitting the wall

- Support of coach and plan

- Students should be building to writing climax

- Closure follows quickly on the heels of climax

11:20–12:00   Mile 8: Student writing on the home stretch
12:00–12:30   Lunch and movement and coaches meet

Be sure to discuss

- Who's in jeopardy of not finishing

- Coaching difficulties

- How to coach when write-a-thoners face hitting the wall

- Importance of slow transitions to ending

- Role of secondary coach to notice something not seen before

- What will those who finish do?

- Fill out certificates for celebration

12:30–12:45   Group coaching session: Resolution

- Quick coaches' check-in and comments on resolutions in books

- Remember to avoid writing "don'ts" (dying, dreaming, and *deus ex machina*)

- After you've read over work, check it out with a coach you haven't spoken to yet

- Share with a classmate: Go through peer evaluation

12:45–1:15   Mile 9: Student writing on resolution, peer evaluation, and a check-out with another coach
1:15–1:25   Student movement, coaches meet, and snack preparation

Coaching questions include:

- Are their story lines making sense?
- Coaching problems that need attention?
- Who's finished?
- Any need for head coaching?
- Who's in danger of not finishing?
- Make sure resolution fits with the problem and with the character; does it avoid the three "don'ts"?
- Determine plan for awards if you've not done so already

| | |
|---|---|
| 1:25– 1:45 | Mile 8: Student writing continues and concludes, peer evaluation, and coaches' check-out |
| 1:45–2:10 | Winners' circle ceremony and party! |

**APPENDIX**

# 10

# *Write-a-thoner's Guide*

 **Write-a-thon: Day 1**

**Goal: Complete Your Story Plan**

Name _____

Character _____

## Mile 1

## Step 1: Begin Building Your Character

Some basic facts about your character:

1. Age

2. Name (nickname?)

3. Male/female; boy/girl; it

What does your character look like?

1. Hair color and eye color

2. Most obvious physical features (e.g., if your character walked in the room, what would people notice first?)

Family life of your character

1. List family members and tell their ages

2. Tell what the family does for fun

3. Name three rules the family has

4. Tell about any pet(s) the family has

## Aid Station: Talk with your coach!

## Mile 1

## Step 2: What is your character like outside home?

1. Who is your character's best friend?

2. Why is this person special?

3. Who is your character's worst enemy?

4. Why does this person hate your character or why does your character hate this person?

**Aid Station: Talk with your coach!**

**Mile 1**

**Step 3: What is your character like inside?**

    A. Strengths and weaknesses

        1. What is your character's greatest strength?

        2. What is your character's greatest weakness?

    B. What does your character act like?

        1. Things that your character likes to do

        2. Things that your character hates to do

**Aid Station: Talk with your coach!**

**Mile 1**

**Step 4: How does your character feel inside?**

    1. What is the most important thing to your character?

    2. What does your character want to be?

    3. What is your character most afraid of?

    4. What is your character most proud of?

    5. Why is your character different than any other character?

    6. What does your character want more than anything?

**Aid Station: Talk with your coach!**

**Mile 2: Conflict**

    1. Describe your character's problem

    2. How does it get in the way of your character's motivation?

**Aid Station: Talk with your coach!**

**Mile 3**

**Plot: Making the problem worse. This is the time to discover the scenes of your story.**

1. How does the problem get worse?

2. How does it get worse again?

3. How does the problem get even worse?

4. How does the problem get even worse?

5. At the climax, or height, of the problem, how does your character take action?

**Aid Station: Talk with your coach!**

**Mile 4: Resolving the Problem**

1. How does your character solve the problem or help solve it? Think of your character's strengths—How can these help now? Is there a character you've put in the story already who can help?

2. What is your solution to the problem?

**Aid Station: Talk with your coach!**

**Homework assignment: The grabber title and grabber first sentence. Bring them with you tomorrow!**

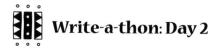 **Write-a-thon: Day 2**

**Goal: A Complete First Draft**

Skip Lines
Coaching and sharing session: Share first lines

## Mile 5:

Write down your grabber first line. Use the one that's going to hook your readers! Give them a little tease about your story, but also give some real information too.

## Mile 6: Setting the Scene
Grabber First Paragraphs

Your first paragraphs should tell who the story's about, where and when it takes place, give a hint about the problem and let us know how your character feels about the situation. Follow your grabber first line with a grabber first paragraph that tells the setting. Read ahead to the First Paragraphs Evaluation to see what you should include in your first paragraphs.

## Aid Station: Talk with your coach! Do not continue until your coach checks off and signs your First Paragraphs Evaluation!

First Paragraphs Evaluation

_____ I can tell when this story takes place

_____ I can tell where this story takes place

_____ I can tell who this story is about

_____ This story makes sense to me

_____ The writer let me know how the main character feels

_____ I'm pretty sure I know the problem in the story

_____ The writer has used at least one metaphor or simile

_____ The writer used at least one description that used the senses

_____ The writer used vivid verbs

My favorite part of this paragraph is _____

_____

Signed _____

## Coaching Session

## Mile 7: The Middle Mile

The middle of your story might have two paragraphs or it might have ten. Check in with a coach at least every three paragraphs. Read ahead to the Middle Miles Evaluation to see what you should include in your middle mile.

## Aid Station: Talk with your coach at the end of every scene! Have your coach complete the Middle Miles Evaluation before you go on to the home stretch

Middle Miles Evaluation

_____ I know what the problem is in the story

_____ I know how the main character feels about or reacts to the problem

_____ I know how other characters feel about or have reacted to the problem

_____ The character takes action in a way that makes sense

_____ The problem is getting worse gradually

_____ The writer is not letting the conflict get solved easily

_____ The writer has used at least one metaphor or simile

_____ The writer used at least one description that used the senses

_____ The writer used vivid verbs

My favorite part of this middle is _____

_____

Signed _____

## Mile 8: The Home Stretch

You're in the home stretch, headed to the finish line. Here are some coaching hints for your resolution:

1. Make the problem even worse

   a. Again, make sure this makes sense with the way it got worse in the step right before

   b. And again, make sure your character has some reaction

   c. Your character might even solve the problem, only to have a new related problem come up (that also makes sense!)

2. The climax: How bad can it get?

   a. Here's your problem as a writer: the more conflict in a story, the more a reader will get grabbed, but don't let it become ridiculous or you'll lose your reader

   b. Try and make the conflict as intense as possible so that your readers will feel the problem your character is having

**Aid Station: Talk with your coach at the end of every scene! Have your coach complete the Home Stretch Evaluation before you go on to the finish line. Read ahead to the Home Stretch Evaluation to see what you should include in your home stretch paragraphs.**

Home Stretch Evaluation

_____ The problems are continuing to get worse

_____ The way the problems get worse still make sense

_____ The way the characters feel about the problems makes sense

_____ The way the characters react to the problems makes sense

_____ Climax: This feels like the last straw to me!

_____ This story still makes sense to me

_____ The main character is still acting in a way that makes sense

_____ The writer has used at least one metaphor or simile

_____ The writer used at least one description that used the senses

_____ The writer used vivid verbs

My favorite part of the home stretch is _____

_____

Signed _____

## Mile 9: The Finish Line and Resolution

Read ahead to the Finish Line Evaluation to see what you should include in your resolution.

## Aid Station: Talk with your coach at the end of every scene! Have your coach complete The Finish Line Evaluation

Now look at the end of your story and evaluate it using these questions:

\_\_\_\_\_ I believe the resolution

\_\_\_\_\_ The resolution makes sense with the rest of the story

\_\_\_\_\_ The way the character solves the problem makes sense

\_\_\_\_\_ The character doesn't die to solve the problem

\_\_\_\_\_ The character doesn't wake up from a dream to solve the problem

\_\_\_\_\_ The character isn't rescued by a character we haven't seen before in the story in order to solve the problem

\_\_\_\_\_ The ending is satisfying (Remember, it doesn't have to be happy!)

\_\_\_\_\_ The writer has used at least one metaphor or simile

\_\_\_\_\_ The writer used at least one description that used the senses

\_\_\_\_\_ The writer used vivid verbs

My favorite part of the ending is _____

_____

Signed _____

Check out with another coach!

Congratulations!

You've successfully completed the Write-a-thon!

# APPENDIX
# 11

# *Certificate of*
# *Completion*

All students who participate in the write-a-thon receive a completed version of the certificate shown on the following page. You may wish to photocopy this certificate onto heavy paper or you may prefer to create a certificate of your own.

**APPENDIX**

# 12

# *Partner Evaluation*

Remember how we read aloud and found words and ideas we wanted to change? Begin draft two by finding a partner who has also finished his or her story.

Decide who will read first.

While the first person reads, the second person listens.

At the end, see if the listener can answer these questions. The listener might make a suggestion that you don't choose to use, but at least listen to what she or he has to say.

\_\_\_\_\_ Are there any parts in the story that don't make sense? Tell me where you get confused.

\_\_\_\_\_ What is your favorite part of my story?

Signed _____

Now switch and listen to your partner's story.

Now look more closely at each part of the story. Look at each other's story bit by bit. First, look at the beginning. You might have to do some rereading to help remember.

## My Story: The Beginning

_____ Does the grabber first sentence grab you? If it doesn't, do you have an idea of how to make it stronger?

_____ Do you understand my character? If you do, tell me these things:

    _____ one thing my character thinks

    _____ what my character's motivation is

    _____ what my character's conflict is

_____ Do you understand the setting of my story?

    _____ I can tell when this story takes place

    _____ I can tell where this story takes place

    _____ I can tell who this story is about

    _____ This story setting makes sense to me

    _____ I'm pretty sure I know the problem in the story

My favorite part of the beginning is _____

_____

Signed _____

## My Story: The Middle

Now look at the middle of your story and evaluate it using these questions:

_____ The problems are getting worse

_____ The way the problems get worse makes sense

_____ The way the characters feel about the problems makes sense

_____ This story makes sense to me

My favorite part of the middle is _____

_____

Signed _____

## My Story: The Ending

Now look at the end of your story and evaluate it using these questions:

_____ I believe the resolution

_____ The resolution makes sense with the rest of the story

_____ The way the character solves the problem makes sense

_____ The character doesn't die to solve the problem

_____ The character doesn't wake up from a dream to solve the problem

_____ The character isn't rescued to solve the problem

_____ The ending is satisfying (remember, it doesn't have to be happy!)

My favorite part of the ending is _____

_____

Signed _____

**APPENDIX**

# 13

# *Working Toward a Third Draft*

Now that you've got the thinking straight all the way through your story, you're ready for draft three. This is a time to really make your writing sing. Go through your manuscript and make a mess of it! Use those skipped lines to add singing to your manuscript. Using the questions below to help you. Begin with the first paragraph.

1. Have I used similes and metaphors to give my readers strong word pictures?

2. Am I repeating words over and over again and losing the chance of using different and stronger words?

3. Have I used strong verbs that really give a sense of the story's action?

4. Have I remembered to include the senses—hearing, sight, smell, taste, and feeling—to make the story more real?

5. Are there places that I can show what my character wants or believes with an action rather than just telling my readers? For example, "Freddie went to the refrigerator for the sixth time and stuffed another peanut butter sandwich in his mouth," instead of "Freddie ate a lot when he was nervous."

After you rewrite your story, read it aloud again to yourself. Pause to feel good about the work you've done to make your story better. Be specific: show yourself at least five places you improved your work. Share your story with a friend and talk about the changes. Have your friend both appreciate your work and show you places you can add more to your story.

# *Publishing*

Many students want their work to be published. Often schools will "publish" books and a copy can be left in the library for sharing. Students may also want to submit their work to some of the magazines listed on the following page. The list was created from Kathy Henderson's *Market Guide for Young Writers: Where and How to Sell What You Write* (Writer's Digest), a wonderful resource that gives lots more information about how to prepare a manuscript, contest, editors' views, etc. I really think every media specialist should purchase a copy for the school. When students submit work, they should send it with a self-addressed stamped envelope so that you will get your manuscript back without costing the company money. Writers don't want to make the people they're submitting to angry!

Picture books of contest winners ages six to nineteen are being published by Landmark Editions. For information, write National Written and Illustrated By Awards Contest for Students, Landmark Editions, Inc., P.O. Box 4469, Kansas City, MO 64127.

*Storyworks* is a national publication about books and writing. It is not only for a place to submit reviews but a literary resource for classrooms. For information contact Storyworks, 730 Broadway, New York, NY 10003. You can call 1-800-631-1586.

 **For Reviews**

Merlyn's Pen: The National Magazine of Student Writing, P.O. Box 910, East Greenwich, RI 02818

Skipping Stones, P.O. Box 3939, Eugene, OR 97403

Stone Soup: The Magazine by Children, P.O. Box 83, Santa Cruz, CA 95063

Writing Right Newsletter, Elmwood Park Publishing, P.O. Box 35132, Elmwood Park, IL 60635

**For Fiction**

The Acorn (for young people K-12), 1530 Seventh Street, Rock Island, IL 61201

Boodle: By Kids, For Kids, P.O. Box 1049, Portland, IN 47371

Creative Kids, Prufrock Press, P.O. Box 8813, Waco, TX 76714-8813

Merlyn's Pen: The National Magazine of Student Writing, P.O. Box 910, East Greenwich, RI 02818

Skipping Stones, P.O. Box 3939, Eugene, OR 97403

Skylark, Purdue University Calumet, 2200 169th Street, Hammond, IN 46323

Spark! 1507 Dana Ave, Cincinnati, OH 45207

Stone Soup: The Magazine by Children, P.O. Box 83, Santa Cruz, CA 95063

The Writer's Slate, P.O. Box 734, Garden City, KS 67846